T0209621

NO CLAIM, NO GAIN

On Your Taxes
and
On God's Promises

Marilou L. Filoteo

authorHOUSE®

AuthorHouse™
1663 Liberty Drive
Bloomington, IN 47403
www.authorhouse.com
Phone: 1 (800) 839-8640

Scripture quotations marked NASB are taken from the New American
Standard Bible®, Copyright © 1960, 1962, 1963, 1968, 1971, 1972, 1973,
1975, 1977, 1995 by The Lockman Foundation. Used by permission.

Published by AuthorHouse 12/02/2019

ISBN: 978-1-7283-3374-8 (sc)
ISBN: 978-1-7283-3372-4 (hc)
ISBN: 978-1-7283-3373-1 (e)

Library of Congress Control Number: 2019917679

Print information available on the last page.

Any people depicted in stock imagery provided by Getty Images are models,
and such images are being used for illustrative purposes only.
Certain stock imagery © Getty Images.

This book is printed on acid-free paper.

This book is dedicated to:

To my parents Papa Max and Mama Salud

And the Whole Family.

PREFACE

Faithful is He Who Promised.

Let us hold unswervingly to the hope we profess,
For He who promised is faithful.

It all started from putting up a website for God. It has been over 11 years since I had this website up, www.GodHearMe.org back in May 2008. I remember it took me a long, long time to develop this. No, not the how but the what. What is purpose of this website, what will be the message, and what are the pages to put up for? I thought I heard Him telling me to do one, which I easily agreed because it was within my skill set at that time as a certified web-and-application developer. I thought that was easy, but I was so wrong. So I asked God again, "Maybe I did not hear you right, Lord, do you want a website from me?" Still a YES, I felt it in my heart. Alright, my spiritual background back then, if these were enough, included: Going to church on Sundays or Saturdays, sometimes reading Bible verses and at times watching TV preachers. With no formal ministry training, this task was definitely difficult if not impossible. Okay, there was the Internet and Google, so anyway I started it. Yes, I struggled, had sleepless nights, and prayed, then ideas came and I got more confident. Before I knew it, wow, I finished it! I showed it to a few friends and family, and they liked it. That was encouraging.

Then together with a prayer partner, we started a prayer group in Facebook called Prayer Warriors of God-Hear-Me. People posting their prayer requests as well as me and other members of the group. I found more prayer partners who were as enthusiastic to serve the Lord as I was. While seeking God's words, I came to learn more and more of His promises and how they affect our daily lives. I want to share them with you thru this book.

Last June, 2019, God Hear Me Ministry LLC was legally formed. It is all in the hands of God where He will take this newly formed organization. An organization whose main purpose is to glorify God and to prosper His Kingdom. God bless you all!

Marilou L. Filoteo

September 1, 2019

ACKNOWLEDGMENTS

Thank you Holy Spirit for the strength and the inspiration to finish this book.

This book is mostly a compilation of Bible Verses using as reference the Biblegateway.com website, including their interpretations. You are an awesome site. Thank you.

On the federal taxes topic, those information are coming from IRS.GOV. Thank you.

On the state taxes topic, those information are coming from MARYLANDTAXES.GOV. Thank you.

On organizing and researching, I would like to thank three people, my two nieces Rosemarie Lazarte and Sally Lazarte, and also to Maritess Maceda Cabahug. Thank you.

To my brother Manuel Lazarte, for helping me with the Introduction. Thank you. To my good friend Cristina Abellana for suggesting edits. Thank you.

To my ever-supportive husband, Vicente. Thank you.

To all who have helped me one way or the other about this book and book writing in general. Thank you.

God bless you all.

INTRODUCTION

First of all, before I introduce myself, I want you to picture this in your mind. Two parents were very distraught, looking at their beautiful almost lifeless little 3 year old girl in a hospital bed, very sick because of her heart condition that was yet to be operated by the specialist doctor.

It was just discovered that her blood was not circulated properly throughout her body thus her breathing was intermittently slow and difficult. She would only have a few years to live if there would be no intervention done due to a hole in right ventricle which pumps blood to her whole little fragile body.

Fast Forward to the Present:

That was me. Now, I live to tell the story of miracles upon miracles in my life and I want to share them with you. I have found my purpose in life, that if I don't share them, I would feel that I failed Him, our Lord Jesus Christ, who has PROMISED me a happy life if I would claim my rights to be in His Kingdom. Like everyone else I am, too, a student eager to learn and make use the promises He offered to us. We will do this together.

My name is Maria Lourdes L. Filoteo. My friends call me Marilou. I am the seventh of nine children, one of only two girls. I grew up in the Philippines, and I must admit, one reason I received so much attention from my parents was that I was born with many health problems. While I was underweight, my heart was enlarged and I had crossed eyes, or strabismus, is a condition in which both eyes do not look at the same place at the same time. When I was three, my kidneys failed, which caused my face, arms and legs to swell up, and I nearly died. Doctors gave up. There was no money for the surgery, which would have been risky anyway, so my parents, devout Christians, had no other option but to cry out to God to spare my life.

Once, when my mother had left me alone in my hospital room for a short while. I was visited by a black priest, who my Mama said was Saint Martin de Porres and who I believe now to have been Jesus. He asked me how I was doing and I said to him that I could not breathe well, and that my head hurt. He gently touched my head. Told me to get up and I did! I thought I could not get up but I was able to. He led me to the window to see the children outside playing on the merry-go-round. I wanted to play too but was unable even to stand up without help at that time. Jesus told me not to worry because I would get better. I did get better and everyone in my family acknowledged that God had done a miracle!

I will say that God has continued to sustain both me and my husband through some difficult times and some health issues. In 2001, I had an open heart surgery called ASD to repair a hole in my heart. I was completely healed. My enlarged heart, now has a normal size. Also, I sat on the US Uniform CPA exams in 2012 and passed all 4 parts. After completing the internship requirements, I became a Certified Public Accountant to the glory and praise of a good and generous God!

All praises and glory belong to God. And yes I claim His promises daily. No Claim. No Gain.

Table of Contents

PART I: TAXES AND DEATH 1

Chapter One: Tax Credits and Deductions 3

What Is a Tax Credit? 5

What Is a Tax Deduction? 6

Credits & Deductions for Businesses 8

PART II: GOD'S PROMISES & BENEFITS 13

Chapter Two: First Things First 14

Have Faith in God 14

Chapter Three: Promises of God – Why Does It Matter? 20

What is a PROMISE? 20

Why is God Making a Promise? 22

Chapter Four: Life Application of the Promises 27

When Things Look Impossible 27

When You Struggle Financially 28

When You Need Healing and Wellness 29

When You Need God's Protection 30

When You Need God's Provision 32

When You Seek His Peace and Joy in Your Life 33

Process Flowchart of His Promises 35

PART III: DAILY BIBLE VERSES GUIDE 38

Chapter Five: Claim Daily and Gain Daily the Benefits 38

Daily Guide – God Promises To Do The Impossible 40

Daily Guide – God Promises To Bless You Financially 41

Daily Guide – God Promises To Heal You 42

Daily Guide – God Promises To Protect You 43

Daily Guide – God Promises To Bring You Blessings 44

Daily Guide – God Promises To Provide for Your Needs 45

Daily Guide – God Promises to Give You Peace & Joy 46

Final Chapter - Claim all the Promises of His Word, and TRUST HIM! 47

PART I: TAXES AND DEATH

Two Certainties

There is a popular saying: The only two things in life that are certain are taxes and death. This is undeniable. There are two stages of this life. In the first stage you are alive and still earning a living and paying taxes on everything you earn. In the second stage you die.

This book has two main objectives. The first is to show you practical ways to save more of the money you earn by helping to avail you of your legal right to claim tax deductions and tax credits. Similarly, because man has both a body and a soul, I am concerned to show you that, just as you have a right to claim income tax credits, the Creator has made even better promises to you than the earthly government, and you have a right to claim His promises in the Bible, every bit as much as you have the right to claim your tax credits and deductions.

While it is a true tragedy that the average person leaves money unclaimed by ignoring his right to claim what the government has promised, it is much more tragic that, although God's promises to His children are amazing and generous, the average Christian lives his or her life failing to take advantage of those promises.

They have salvation by Jesus's finished work on the cross, and they will go to be with Him when they die, or when Jesus returns. But while we have been promised an abundant life, and a victorious life where we as God's children are more than conquerors, they fail to claim God's promises and struggle through life, harassed by Satan, feeling defeated, and living far short of the abundant life that is promised.

God has given principles and promises, but we leave them on the table just as we do our tax credits and deductions, and so we don't get everything God would say is ours for the taking. This must stop. It is my desire to help you to see what God has for you, and show you how the Bible says you can grasp these great and awesome promises!

Chapter One: Tax Credits and Deductions

The majority of this book will be about God's wonderful promises in the Bible, and how to claim them. But because I am a Certified Public Accountant by trade, I will start by listing the income tax credits and deductions. Part of being a child of God and a follower of His Son, Jesus Christ, is being a good steward. A steward is a manager. The Christian understands that nothing we have is our own. It all belongs to God. In 1 Corinthians 4:2, it says ...it is required of stewards that they be found faithful. God endows us with gifts, talents, resources and opportunities, and He expects us to make the most of what He has given us. We consider all of it His. What we have is from Him, and for Him.

Jesus told several parables that illustrated the point. In one, he said that the Kingdom of God is like a man that went away and entrusted his property to managers. The master returns to demand an account for how his property was managed (Matthew 25:14-28). Jesus makes it clear that it is according to what one is given that one will be judged. The servant with five talents (a talent was a sum of money) was expected to produce more than the servant who was given two, or only one talent. No one was punished for failure in their endeavors to multiply the talents, only for failing to endeavor at all.

The one who left unclaimed all the benefits of serving the rich and generous master, was considered in the end to be wicked and lazy and sent away. God is merciful. If you have received Jesus as your Lord and Savior you will be with him for eternity. But the quality of your experience both here, and in the next life will be determined by this principle of stewardship. God's promises are there. It is your decision whether to claim them or not. No claim, no gain.

Whether you consider yourself to have been given little, or much, the expectation is that you will make the most of it, by claiming what is yours, because by doing that, you are really claiming what is God's. Consider even claiming all your tax deductions to be good stewardship, so that you can use God's money in even better ways. The Bible is clear, God's creation runs on stewardship. He created man and woman and entrusted them to rule and make something of what He gave them on His behalf (Genesis 1:26-28). So in this sense, even claiming your tax benefits is obedience to Him.

So what are they? A tax deduction is a dollar amount that the IRS allows you to subtract from your adjusted gross income, or AGI, making your taxable income lower. The lower your taxable income, the lower your tax bill.

What Is a Tax Credit?

Subtract tax credits from the amount of tax you owe. There are two types of tax credits:

- A nonrefundable tax credit means you get a refund only up to the amount you owe.
- A refundable tax credit means you get a refund, even if it's more than what you owe.

A tax credit is a dollar-for-dollar reduction in your actual tax bill. A few credits are refundable, which means if you owe, for instance, $250 in taxes but qualify for a $1000 credit, you'll get a check for the difference of $750. Most tax credits, however are not refundable. For this reason, the tax credit can be a much greater benefit than the deduction. What follows is a list of the most popular types of each kind of benefit.

Credits for Individuals

Family and Dependent Credits

- EITC = Earned Income Tax Credit
- Child & Dependent Care Credit
- Adoption Credit
- Child Tax Credit
- Credit for the Elderly and/or Disabled

Income and Savings Credits

- EITC = Earned Income Tax Credit
- Retirement Saver's Credit
- Foreign Tax Credit
- Excess Social Security and RRTA Tax Withheld

- Credit for Tax on Undistributed Capital Gains
- Nonrefundable Credit for Prior Year Minimum Tax – Individuals, Estates & Trust
- Credit to Holders of Tax Credit Bonds

Homeowner Credits

- Residential Energy Efficient Property Credit
- Nonbusiness Energy Property Credit
- Low-Income Housing Credit (for Owners)

Health Care Credits

- Premium Tax Credit (Affordable Care Act)
- Health Coverage Tax Credit

Education Credits

- American Opportunity Credit and Lifetime Learning Credit

What Is a Tax Deduction?

Subtract tax deductions from your income before you figure the amount of tax you owe.

Deductions for Individuals

Work Related Deductions

- Employee Business Expenses
- Home Office
- Business Entertainment Expenses

Itemized Deductions

- Deductible Taxes
- Property Tax
- Real Estate Tax
- Sales Tax
- Charitable Contributions
- Gambling Loss
- Miscellaneous Expenses
- Interest Expense
- Home Mortgage Interest
- Union/Club/Moving Expenses

Education Deductions

- Student Loan Interest
- Work-Related Educational Expenses
- Teacher Educational Expenses

Health Care Deductions

- Medical and Dental Expenses
- Health Savings Account (HSA)

Investment Related Deductions

- Sale of Home
- Individual Retirement Arrangements (IRAs)
- Capital Losses
- Bad Debt

Credits & Deductions for Businesses

- Manufacturers' Energy Efficient Appliance Credit
  Act Section 305 - Modifications of Energy Efficient Appliance Credit for Appliances Produced After 2007

- Plug-In Electric Drive Vehicle Credit - Internal Revenue Code Section 30D provides a credit for Qualified Plug-in Electric Drive Motor Vehicles including passenger vehicles and light trucks.

- Research Credit
  Guidelines and audit technique guide are provided for field examiners on the examination of Research Credit cases.

- Deducting Business Expenses
  Find out what qualifies as a deductible business expense, including depreciation.

- Abusive Tax Shelters and Transactions
  The Internal Revenue Service has a comprehensive strategy in place to combat abusive tax shelters and transactions. This strategy includes guidance on abusive transactions, regulations governing tax shelters, a hotline for taxpayers to use to report abusive technical transactions, and enforcement activity against abusive tax shelter promoters and investors.

State Tax Benefits

While you should check with your local and state revenue offices to become aware of the particular benefits for your localities. Here are some of the more common state tax benefits, most of which are credits. To name a few:

- Child Tax Credit
- Tax Paid in Other States
- Education Savings Plan
- Low Income credits
- Teachers Incentive credits
- Two (2) Family Income
- Student Loan/ Debt relief Program
- More depending in your location …

These tax credits need to be claimed to gain the benefits of lower taxes. NO CLAIM, NO GAIN.

So be a good manager of the finances that God has entrusted to you. The overarching principle in scripture is that God waits to see you handle a little before He entrusts you with a lot. Take responsibility for whatever you have been given.

It is a blessing for which to be thankful. It is being responsible and faithful to get the most money back on your taxes that you are able to.

It is your right to use them.

Do not leave these valuable
Tax Benefits unclaimed.

Shown above are USA based Tax Law. There should be similar tax provisions whereever you reside in the world. Be aware of the tax credits available to you. The above just are examples to illustrate that benefits have to be claimed for you gain on them.

We sampled about 30 countries below from around the world to look at how they treat their tax deductions and tax credits. Remember different countries, different terminologies.

To understand the Country Tax Credit Table below let us look at each column.

Column 1 is the Country name.

Column 2 is whether deductions against personal and buisness income are allowed. Deduction can be seen as Allowances, Allowed Expenses, Authorized Expenses and Exceptions. YES means they have deducctions on their taxes to reduce the taxable income. And they must be explicitly itemized or using some kind of standard deductions.

NO INFO means that on their websites, it cannot be determined if their tax code allows them. NO INFO also means ask your local tax professionals.

Column 3 is whether they have TO BE CLAIMED or lose them. NO INFO means that there is no information found on the website about tax credits. Tax Credit term equivalents are: Exemptions, Excluded, Special Treatments and Specific Credits their tax codes provided.

Note that the above are findings based on their websites limited information. **No extensive reseach and / or studies done on them to generate an income tax reporting.** Especially also on those countries that have non-English words.

Collumn 4 are the links for each country's revenue / tax centers, to help in your understanding. As of time of writing, they were active in the Internet. You may want to copy and paste in your browsers.

COUNTRY TAX CREDITS TABLE

Country	Deductions	Tax Credits	Links
Argentina	YES	NO INFO	http://www.afip.gov.ar
Australia	YES	TO BE CLAIMED	https://www.ato.gov.au/
Canada	YES	TO BE CLAIMED	https://www.canada.ca/en/revenue-agency.html
China	YES	NO INFO	http://www.chinatax.gov.cn/
Denmark	YES	TO BE CLAIMED	https://skat.dk/skat.aspx?oid=2244281
Ethiopia	NO INFO	NO INFO	http://www.mor.gov.et/
Finland	YES	TO BE CLAIMED	https://www.vero.fi/en/search/?query=DEDUCTION
France	YES	TO BE CLAIMED	https://www.expatica.com/fr/finance/taxes/
Germany	YES	NO INFO	https://www.bzst.de/EN/Federal_Central_Tax_Office
Iceland	YES	NO INFO	https://www.island.is/en/finance/taxes
India	YES	TO BE CLAIMED	https://finmin.nic.in/
Indonesia	YES	NO INFO	http://www.pajak.go.id/
Ireland	YES	TO BE CLAIMED	https://revenue.ie/en/Home.aspx
Italy	YES	TO BE CLAIMED	https://www.agenziaentrate.gov.it/portale/
Japan	YES	TO BE CLAIMED	https://www.nta.go.jp/english/
Kenya	YES	NO INFO	https://www.kra.go.ke/en/
Mexico	YES	NO INFO	https://www.gob.mx/sre
Netherland	YES	TO BE CLAIMED	https://www.government.nl/topics/income-tax
New Zealand	YES	TO BE CLAIMED	https://www.ird.govt.nz/
Israel	YES	TO BE CLAIMED	https://taxes.gov.il/Pages/HomePage.aspx
Norway	YES	TO BE CLAIMED	http://www.finans.dep.no/
Philippines	YES	TO BE CLAIMED	http://government.ru/
Puerto Rico	YES	TO BE CLAIMED	http://www.hacienda.gobierno.pr/
Russia	NO INFO	NO INFO	http://government.ru/
Singapore	YES	TO BE CLAIMED	https://www.iras.gov.sg/irashome/default.aspx
South Africa	YES	TO BE CLAIMED	http://www.sars.gov.za/
Spain	YES	TO BE CLAIMED	https://www.agenciatributaria.es/
Sweden	YES	TO BE CLAIMED	http://skatteverket.se/
Switzerland	YES	TO BE CLAIMED	https://www.estv.admin.ch/estv/de/home.html
United Kingdom	YES	TO BE CLAIMED	https://www.gov.uk/topic/personal-tax/income-tax

NO INFO means that on their websites, it cannot be determined if their tax code allows them. NO INFO also means ask your local tax professionals.

Column 3 is whether they have TO BE CLAIMED or lose them.

PART II: GOD'S PROMISES & BENEFITS

Tax code has tax credits written down to be claimed and get benefits from them. In the same way, God's code is found in His Word. The benefits in this God' promises are found in scripture. Each benefit will have its own chapter that is meant to be read on a specific day of the week, and will be accompanied by a prayer for the day. What follows is a brief description of each promise.

Monday	Impossible
Tuesday	Financial
Wednesday	Healing
Thursday	Protection
Friday	General
Saturday	Provision
Sunday	Peace & Joy

God Promises to Do the Impossible for You
God Promises to Bless You Financially
God Promises to Heal You
God Promises to Protect You
God Promises to Bless You
God Promises to Provide Your Needs
God Promises to Give You Peace & Joy

Chapter Two: First Things First

Before we begin mining scripture for God's promises, I want to make sure that we are starting from the same place. The rest of this book will assume you are a fellow believer. Many of the promises of God are born out of the way He has designed His universe to work, and so they are based on principles that will even serve the nonbeliever. This is because of God's will to bless His creation. He is gracious and makes His sun rise on the evil and on the good, and sends rain on the just and on the unjust. All blessings are from God. Even the unbeliever who does not acknowledge God owes thanks for every breath he breathes. God is kind and patient. He will wait, and while He waits He will bless. He is the source of all life and all good things.

However, claiming His promises presupposes belief.

Have Faith in God

The question is, how do you get this eternal life? How do you become saved? How do you get restored back to God in a right relationship? The answer is faith.

What if you are aware of the promise but doubt the reliability of the person who gave it? The result would be that you will not take the promise seriously. As it were, my duty now is to tell you few things about God as related to His promises so that your faith might increase. Bible is the record of God's dealings with men written by men as they were inspired by the Holy Ghost. So I will be taking you through the personality of God concerning his promises as revealed in the bible.

For you to benefit from the promises of God you need to really believe in Him. 'Believe in God' 'have faith in God' are common phrases you hear every time especially among the religious people. Maybe among those who attend church only on Christmas too. But what exactly does it mean to believe or have faith in God? It means to believe in God's character. To believe that God cannot lie; He meant whatever He says. To believe that God is alive; many do not really believe this. They thought it is all fiction. It also means to believe in God's unchanging nature. Moreover, it means to believe that God has power to do anything he promises no matter who does not want it to happen. Furthermore, it means to believe that He is willing and ready to do all He wishes. And finally, it is to believe that none can reverse whatever He does.

Now let us look at these characters in detail.

God cannot lie.

Each time you doubt God's promise you call Him a liar. This is one thing God cannot do – He cannot lie. He does not joke. Let us look at the testimonies of people in the bible. It says

God is not a man that He should lie.

Has God promised you anything? Perhaps you read a passage in the bible that appears to address your situation. You can be sure that He will fulfill it. It is impossible for God to lie.

God cannot die.

It may surprise you that many do not believe that God exist, despite the enumerable facts from nature that surround us. The whole earth is full of his Glory. Halleluiah! Some believe that there was once a God but He is no longer interested in the affair of men. They said God has retired. Maybe your faith too in the existence of God is also shaky. God is alive. God is not dead and He has not retired. He rules in the affairs of men! You need to believe this if you must experience the reality of His promises.

God does not change.

Change is the only constant thing among men. But God does not change. He is from eternity to eternity. What He was 5,000 years ago that is what He is now and that is what He will be forever. "Jesus Christ the same yesterday and today and forever" Hebrew 13:8.

It follows that if God does not change then His promises also cannot change. This is important for you to know since many of the promises of God in the bible were written thousands of years ago.

God is the all Almighty and all Powerful.

Today's believers need not fear. All power has been given to our redeemer and savior – Jesus Christ. Do you like working for God, doing one thing or the other for God but you are afraid? Do not fear! All power in heaven and on earth has been given to Jesus he will make sure that you accomplish whatsoever he has committed into your hand.

God is willing.

Having established the fact that God can do everything, the question now is whether or not He is willing to do it for you. You have read or heard what wonders He did for other people. And you are wondering if He would do the same for you.

This feeling or question is often informed by our fear of unworthiness. Sin particularly will make anyone to want to hide from the face of a Holy God. There are many other things that can create this feeling of unworthiness. The point is that it does not matter how you feel, if you believe in God's promise and fulfils the conditions, God is more than willing to do it for you. At times the condition may be as simple as having faith, other times, it could requires repentance and restitution. But one thing is certain; God is willing to fulfill His promises in your life.

God is ready.

Now that we know that God is willing another question is that is He ready now? One can be willing but not ready. At times, people are willing to do certain thing but they are not ready. This could be as a result of their inability at that point in time. God is not limited in time and space. He is able to do all that He wants to do. God is up to the task in your life, He is willing and ready right now. You can be healed right now. You can receive provision right now. You can be strengthened right now. You can receive deliverance right now.

He is ready to forgive you of all sins and wrong doings. You do not need to carry the burden about. And it does not matter how grievous. Come, all things are now ready!

No one can undo His work.

At times we fear that human or Satan will take away or undo what God has done for us.

This fear is unfounded. Because it is written that none can undo what God has done. When I act, who can reverse it?" Isaiah 43:13. Therefore, you need to believe that His promises for you are irreversible. Another interpretation says that no one can snatch you from Him or stand in His way.

You know it is ridiculous (for lack of a better term) to think that someone or something will reverse whatever God Almighty did for us.

God hates unbelief.

As believers if there is anything to fear, that thing is unbelief. That is your greatest enemy not human or devil. Unbelief is the only thing that will not make the promises of God to be yes and amen in your life. As truthful, powerful, willing, ready as God is, unbelief will limit His working in any life. We read in the Matthew 13:58 "Now He did not do many mighty works there because of their unbelief".

In sum, it has been said that promises are as good as the giver. Having shown you few things about the person of God, you will agree with me that His promises are worth believing. You can lay hold of any of His promises related to your circumstances and be sure that He will perform it. It is suffice to tell you that while God is faithful, we have roles to play in obtaining His promises. I know you are eager to discover what exactly you need to do to claim these promises. Follow me as we discover these requisites in next chapter.

In Romans 4, says that Abraham believed God and it was counted to him as righteousness. Some translations say it was reckoned to him, others say it was credited to him.

For our purposes in this book, understand that of all the benefits, the promises of God, this is the very first credit, and it is the most wonderful credit of them all. Romans 3 says it is a righteousness apart from the law, by faith that has manifested in Jesus Christ.

This is astounding.

How do you receive this credit? By believing.

Do you believe that you, like our first parents, are in need of help from God?

Have you experienced the shame and guilt of your existence on this fallen world?

Have you noticed that your life is not what you hoped it would be because living it on your own strength just isn't working?

But because of Christ, we who believe and put our faith in Him are born again to live forever because of God's merciful accounting! He has paid the price for our sin. He has covered our shame with not our death, but the death of his Son. Praise God!

So if you have never put your faith in God, do it now.

 You may pray this way:

Lord Jesus, I know that I am a sinner, and I have sinned in my life. I want to be saved and live with you for eternity. I put my faith in you because I believe your death on the cross was enough to save me from hell and to wash away my sin. From this day forward, I want to learn to be like you, Lord Jesus. I want to follow you. Give me the strength and knowledge to do that. I want to love and serve you all the days of my life. Amen.

So for the rest of the book, I will detail how to make the most of the following benefits and promises of God, how to claim them because No Claim, No Gain.

Chapter Three: Promises of God – Why Does It Matter?

God's promises are written commitment from no other than the Most High God. Joshua 21:45 says, Not one of the good promises that the LORD had made to the house of Israel failed—all of them came about.

If God says He will do something, than He will. If God says He will refrain from doing something, He will.

How Many Promises Are There in The Bible?

From different sources, different answer. In one source it said 5,467 Divine Promises. All sources agree that God's promises are irrevocable. Of the thousands of God's promises, Caleb in the Bible hang on to one promise. Thru no fault of his, he waited 40 years to receive his reward, entering the promise land.

What is a PROMISE?

The dictionary definition goes as follows:

1. A declaration that something will or will not be done.

2. An express assurance on which expectation is to be based.

A promise is usually given about something to be fulfilled and that is not a daily occurrence, not obvious. It is a special thing. It is a gift of God.

God promises us things that will be challenged or even disbelief. God does not promise obvious things like the sun rises and sun sets. Instead, He promises us that He will never leave us nor forsake us, because He knew at some point in our lives, we may think and feel that like He is not there. This gets harder to believe and understand when we are suffering. Our hearts will have doubts, discouraged and seems look like He has forgotten us and left us on our own. Be assured that no matter what challenged we are in, no matter what comes our way, He promised that He will never leave us, nor will He ever forsake us. Amen.

God Makes Two Types of Promises

Unconditional Promises.

This is a promise that is made without attaching any conditions whatsoever. A good example of His resolute determination to carry out His purposes, no matter what individuals may do or think, is an incident which took place as God was about to lead the children of Israel into Canaan.

Other unconditional promises:

Acts 10:36 … there is peace with God through Jesus Christ, who is Lord of all. Matthew 19:26 … with God everything is possible.

Matthew 11:28 … When you are weary and carry heavy burdens, Jesus will give you rest

Matthew 11:30… For my yoke is easy to bear, and the burden I give you is light. James 1:17… Whatever is good and perfect is a gift from God our Father

2 Cor. 3:17 Now the Lord is the Spirit, and where the Spirit of the Lord is, there is freedom.

Conditional Promises.

This type of promise is subject to certain qualifications or requirements. Perhaps that promise was conditional and we do not meet the requirements.

This is why it is important to understand the context of a promise. You have to pray for discernment. It is not wise to pick a random promise and make it for your own.

God's blessing upon our lives are not automatic. When we obey God's commands and truthful in heart, we begin to see the rewards of God's blessing upon our lives.

The scripture is full of promises, so many of them that we need to determine if these promises are conditional. Read the full context of the promise.

God has promised to give us the desires of our heart but they are conditional. Like knowing someone and you delight to be with that person always. Then God will respond then delight in giving us those desires in our hearts.

If you want to benefit from these promises, look at the conditions attached and obey them.

Why is God Making a Promise?

In the earlier chapter we talked about the Characters of God. He is nothing like us. He is God. But why is He making a promise to you and me. A mere human. As I get closer to Him and follow Jesus, I found six (6) reasons why.

One. Basis for Our Faith in God

Unlike man, God does not flip-flop with His words. He never changes His mind at any time. God is not like us humans, He is God. He does not change His mind. Because of this it establishes our faith on Him.

Question: Has he ever spoken and failed to act? Has he ever promised and not carried it through?

Answer: No

All God's promises to Abraham He fulfilled. I promise that you will be the father of many nations. Genesis 17:4

Christ is our Yes Lord! to God's promises

For Jesus Christ, the Son of God, does not waver between Yes and No. He is the one whom Silas, Timothy, and John the Baptist preached to you, and as God's ultimate Yes, he always does what he says. For all of God's promises have been fulfilled in Christ with a resounding Yes! And through Christ, our Amen (which means Yes) ascends to God for his glory.

Two. Demonstrates God's Faithfulness

God is so faithful that anyone who seeks Him can find Him. Faith is a gift, but even a gift must be opened to be enjoyed. As we implement our faith, we begin to realize more and more about God's faithfulness to us.

God the Father who allowed His Son Jesus Christ to live us and be among us. He promised this way before Jesus came to earth. He fulfilled this promise by the birth of our Lord Jesus. God is faithful.

Three. Encourages Us During Hard Times.

God will not withhold what is good

God's plans for all of us are always good, and His promises are always good (see Jeremiah 29:11). These good things He will never withhold from those who carefully pursue Him and His Word!

Also 1 Corinthians 10:13 He will protect us and we cannot be tempted beyond what we can bear. But when you are tempted, He will also provide a way out so you can stand up under it.

As a young man, David was a shepherd and he fought ferocious animals preying upon his flock -- the bear and the lion. He went out after it and struck it, and killed it.

Though challenges come to our lives, we do not know why God allowed them. He will protect us beyond what we can bear. You just have to trust in His will.

Four. Leads Us in the Right Path

When you make this full surrender with God, it is now His job to take full and complete care of you in every detail of your life – including finding the next new job that He will want you to move into.

There is not an area or detail in your life that God will not be willing to help you out with –

no matter how small or trivial you think it may be.

You simply have to learn how to have patience during these waiting periods.

In the meantime, God will make sure and arrange that you have enough money and support coming in to help keep you afloat until this next job comes through. This is where you have to learn how to have complete faith in the Lord to do all of this for you.

God never promised it would be an easy ride.

But He did promise He will never leave you and you are not alone in your journey.

Five. To Have a Deep Communion with God

As Christians, we are called to love our brothers and sisters in Christ. First, let us understand how we are drawn into a life-giving relationship with God himself. You are secure in your union with Christ Jesus, and this union makes communion with God the Father a joyful possibility. Be assured this union will flourish and gain strength in communion with him.

In Deuteronomy 6:4-5 He commanded you to love your God with all your heart and with all your soul and with all your might. He wants to be in communion with you. Your heart must be united in His love.

In Deuteronomy 7:7-9, show us that His lovingkindness to a thousandth generation with those who love Him and keep His commandments; He is faithful.

Six. For the Glory of God

Honor, Praise, Magnify, Distinction - all are words synonymous with GLORY. As a manifestation of the work of His hands, all creation brings glory to God. In Genesis 1:31 we read, God saw all that He had made, and it was very good. And there was evening, and there was morning-the sixth day.

In Psalm 138:5 …. Come let us sing for the glory of the LORD is great!

In Psalm 19:1 says the heavens declare the glory of God; the skies proclaim the work of his hands. God's very work praises Him and brings Him glory. Amen.

Glory to God is displayed through His mighty actions.

Psalm 111:3 says glorious and majestic are His deeds, and His righteousness endures forever. No one can accomplish what God can. He is above and beyond our comprehension.

A more famous verse about His glory, is a command from God:

1 Corinthians 10:31-33

Whether, then, you eat or drink or whatever you do, do all to the glory of God. Give no offense either to Jews or to Greeks or to the church of God; just as I also please all men in all things, not seeking my own profit but the profit of the many, so that they may be saved.

Amen.

Chapter Four: Life Application of the Promises

When Things Look Impossible

God's Promise: For Nothing is Impossible with God

In Luke 1:37, Mary, the mother of Jesus is told by the angel Gabriel that nothing is impossible with God. When Jesus' disciples asked him how a rich man could possibly enter the Kingdom of Heaven, he said with people this is impossible, but with God all things are possible.

In Job 42:2, Job says to God - I know that you can do all things, and that no purpose of yours can be thwarted.

Now, what do you think it means when it says all things are possible? What is encompassed in all? I'll tell you. It means all things!

What do you think it means when it says that nothing is impossible. It means nothing is impossible!

God is the one who designed the universe.

He designed the laws of physics, the laws of nature, all of it.

When Jesus walked on water, or caused fish and bread to materialize, it is because God is the master of all reality and can manipulate it at will.

God can do all things!

Speak the words of God in your prayer.

Mondays are the days we assigned that we claim His promises to do what we thought was impossible.

When You Struggle Financially

God's Promise: His Plan is To Prosper You and Not Harm You

God promises in the Bible to bless you financially. If you are a generous person, and if you trust Him, He will do it.

Below are where God strongly promised for your financial blessings.

- In Malachi 3:10 says - Bring the whole tithe into the storehouse, so that there may be food in My house, and test Me now in this, says the Lord of hosts, if I will not open for you the windows of heaven and pour out for you a blessing until it overflows.

  How much is God asking from us?
  10% of your income. Giving tithes and financial management are spiritual issues as well not just a financial issue.

- And what is God's Plan for you?
  His answer is found In Jeremiah 29:11

  For I know the plans I have for you, declares the LORD, - plans to prosper you and not to harm you, plans to give you hope and a future.

- 2 Corinthians 9:6-8 says - Now this I say, he who sows sparingly will also reap sparingly, and he who sows bountifully will also reap bountifully. Each one must do just as he has purposed in his heart, not grudgingly or under compulsion, for God loves a cheerful giver. And God is able to make all grace abound to you, so that always having all sufficiency in everything, you may have an abundance for every good deed.

- In Proverbs 3:9-10 says - Honor the Lord from your wealth and from the first of all your produce; so your barns will be filled with plenty and your vats will overflow with new wine.

These verses and many other promise financial blessing as we follow Him and live according to His ways and Biblical wisdom. When a Christian trusts the Lord with his or her money, and follows God with a devoted heart, God promises to bless them financially.

Tuesdays are the days we assigned to claim His promises to bless you financially

When You Need Healing and Wellness

God's Promise: He Wants To Heal You

It is His will to heal you.

When you pray, do not say if it is Your will Lord. Because it is His will to give you healing. Just claim it. Jeremiah 17:14 says - Heal me, O Lord, and I will be healed;

Save me and I will be saved, for You are my praise.

In His three year ministry before He took your place on the cross, our Lord Jesus showed that God is a healing God. In Matthew 8 says - When evening came, they brought to Him many who were demon-possessed; and He cast out the spirits with a word, and healed all who were ill.

Notice, ALL were healed, not just a few. Because God's will is to heal you.

This was to fulfill what was spoken through Isaiah the prophet: He Himself took our infirmities and carried away our diseases.

I myself can say this: If God did not heal me I would not be here writing this book.

Every day is good day to claim the healing promises. Here we assigned Wednesdays as the day that we claim His promises to do healing.

When You Need God's Protection

God's Promise: He Keeps You Safe in a Dangerous World

Psalm 46 says God is our refuge and strength, A very present help in trouble.

Therefore we will not fear, though the earth should change And though the mountains slip into the heart of the sea; Though its waters roar and foam,

Though the mountains quake at its swelling pride.

The Bible abounds with promises of God's protection for His people.

In the 23rd Psalm, verse 4 it says - Even though I walk through the valley of the shadow of death, I fear no evil, for You are with me; Your rod and Your staff, they comfort me.

Psalm 121 I will lift up my eyes to the mountains; From where shall my help come?

2 My help comes from the Lord, Who made heaven and earth.

3 He will not allow your foot to slip; He who keeps you will not slumber.

4 Behold, He who keeps Israel

Will neither slumber nor sleep.

5 The Lord is your keeper;

The Lord is your shade on your right hand.

6 The sun will not smite you by day,

Nor the moon by night.

7 The Lord will protect you from all evil; He will keep your soul.

8 The Lord will guard your going out and your coming in From this time forth and forever.

There is absolutely no doubt that God promises to protect His people. Claim this promise!

We need protection every second of our life, pray daily for protection.

We assigned Thursday as the day that we claim His promise to protection.

When You Need God's Blessings

God's Promise: He Gives You His Blessings

On Fridays we pray for God's blessing in general. He has so many ways He wants to bless us and care for us. We could not possibly think to pray for all of them, so we will pray for Him to bless us in all the ways that He is able.

The Lord will bless His people because He loves them. Follow His ways and trust Him for this blessing. Blessings comes in many forms not just financial. Examples are Divine Intervention – not luck but His intervention. Divine Connections, have you wondered why you meet good people in your life. What about not getting sick, this is a blessing too.

Fridays we assigned to claim His promises of continued blessings.

When You Need God's Provision

God's Promise: Trust in His Provision

In Matthew 6 Jesus says it all. Long and detailed. He knows our fears and promises this unconditionally.

- For this reason I say to you, do not be worried about your life, as to what you will eat or what you will drink; nor for your body, as to what you will put on. Is not life more than food, and the body more than clothing? Look at the birds of the air, that they do not sow, nor reap nor gather into barns, and yet your heavenly Father feeds them. Are you not worth much more than they? And who of you by being worried can add a single hour to his life? And why are you worried about clothing? Observe how the lilies of the field grow; they do not toil nor do they spin, yet I say to you that not even Solomon in all his glory clothed himself like one of these. But if God so clothes the grass of the field, which is alive today and tomorrow is thrown into the furnace, will He not much more clothe you?

You of little faith! Do not worry then, saying, 'What will we eat?' or 'What will we drink?' or 'What will we wear for clothing?' For the Gentiles eagerly seek these things; for your heavenly Father knows that you need all these things.

God First. - But seek first His kingdom and His righteousness, and all these things will be added to you. In this wonderful promise, Jesus says that God absolutely will provide for us if we seek His Kingdom first.

> Psalm 37:25 says I have been young and now I am old, Yet
> I have not seen the righteous forsaken
> Or his descendants begging bread.
> They pray for provision because they trust in the Provider.

Saturdays are the days we assigned to claim His promises of continued provisions.

When You Seek His Peace and Joy in Your Life

God's Promise: Peace & Joy – The Fruit of the Spirit

Finally, we will pray on the Lord's Day and ask the Father for peace and joy. Once again the Bible is the foundation of our claim.

Colossians 3:15 - Let the peace of Christ rule in your hearts, to which indeed you were called in one body; and be thankful.

We were called to the Peace of Christ, our Lord and Savior. This one you should keep in heart.

John 14:27 - Peace I leave with you; My peace I give to you; not as the world gives do I give to you. Do not let your heart be troubled, nor let it be fearful.

Jesus' promise is that He leaves us with His peace. We can claim this promise and let go of the trouble and the fear in our hearts.

Look at Isaiah 26:3 --- You will keep in perfect peace those whose minds are steadfast, because they trust in you. 4 Trust in the Lord forever, for the Lord, the Lord himself, is the Rock eternal.

Psalm 4:8 says -- In peace I will both lie down and sleep, For You alone, O Lord, make me to dwell in safety.

Simply put, the Lord is our peace, and the Lord gives us peace. Claim this promise and have a tranquil heart.

Sundays are the days that we assigned to claim His promise of Peace and Joy in our lives.

Process Flowchart of His Promises

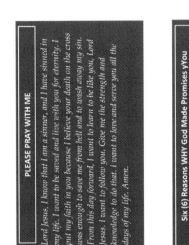

You Are a Believer

HAVE FAITH IN GOD

God cannot lie
God cannot die
God does not change
God is Almighty & Powerful
God is willing
God is ready
No one can undo His work
God hates unbelief

PLEASE PRAY WITH ME

Lord Jesus, I know that I am a sinner, and I have sinned in my life. I want to be saved and live with you for eternity. I put my faith in you because I believe your death on the cross was enough to save me from hell and to wash away my sin. From this day forward, I want to learn to be like you, Lord Jesus. I want to follow you. Give me the strength and knowledge to do that. I want to love and serve you all the days of my life. Amen.

What is a Promise?

WHY DOES IT MATTER?

Unconditional Promises
Conditional Promises
Why God Made Promises?

Six (6) Reasons WHY God Made Promises yYou

1. *Basis for your faith in God*
2. Demonstrates His faithfulness
3. Encourages you during hard times
4. Leads you in the right path
5. To have a deep communion with God
6. For the Glory of God

Life Application of The Promises

The Challenges of Life

When Things Look Impossible
When You Struggle Financially
When You Need Healing and Wellness
When You Need God's Protection
When You Need God's Blessings
When You Need God's Provision
When You Seek His Peace and Joy in Your Life

The Promises of God

God Promises to Do the Impossible for You
God Promises to Bless You Financially
God Promises to Heal You
God Promises to Protect You
God Promises to Bless You
God Promises to Provide Your Needs
God Promises to Give You Peace & Joy

To Claim His Promises You must have a HEART for God.

A Believer.

The process begins with a HEART

You questioned yourself WHY should I have FAITH in God ?

The anser is for you to PRAY to receive this Gift of Faith.

You questioned WHAT is PROMISE ?

There are conditional and unconditional promises to talk to God of His Word.

But WHY God made PROMISES. There are 6 reasons.

You questioned HOW do I apply these promises to my LIFE ?

7 days a week, you have to CLAIM DAILY, GAIN DAILY.

NO CLAIM, NO GAIN.

PART III: DAILY BIBLE VERSES GUIDE

Chapter Five: Claim Daily and Gain Daily the Benefits

Monday	Impossible
Tuesday	Financial
Wednesday	Healing
Thursday	Protection
Friday	General
Saturday	Provision
Sunday	Peace & Joy

I hope that in this book you have seen the value in following God with your whole life, and loving Him with your whole heart. A relationship with Jesus is without a doubt the number one best reason to pray every day and claim His promises.

Be patient as you pray and learn to trust God wholly. I have had prayers that were answered immediately, and I have had prayers that God had a reason to allow me to wait for. He is a kind, and wise Father, and He makes no mistakes. His ultimate goal for us is that we would look and act like His blessed Son, Jesus. There is not one single hardship, not one moment of suffering, not one setback that the LORD will not use to teach us, grow us, and bless us.

My prayer for you is that you get everything God has for you in this life, but especially in the next!

Dear reader, surrender your life to Jesus if you have not already. Ask Him to make His home in you and transform you. Have the courage to say whatever it takes, be glorified in my life. Claim all the promises of His Word, and TRUST HIM!

Claim His Promises Daily and pray in Jesus name. AMEN.

Daily Guide – God Promises To Do The Impossible

Our Prayer

Father God, we are facing difficult challenges in our lives today and we believe that You can save us because nothing is too difficult for You to do. It is impossible for us to find the right path without Your Divine intervention. We claim these promises that you can do the impossible for us for nothing is too hard for you to do and we have faith in You.

In the name of Jesus we pray. Amen

God Promises To Do The Impossible

1st Monday of January

Date: _____

2nd Monday of January

Date: _____

Ecclesiastes 3:11 New American Standard Bible (NASB)

God Set Eternity in the Heart of Man

[11] He has made everything appropriate in its time. He has also set eternity in their heart, yet so that man will not find out the work which God has done from the beginning even to the end.

Isaiah 65:17 New American Standard Bible (NASB)

[17] "For behold, I create new heavens and a new earth; And the former things will not be remembered or come to mind.

3rd Monday of January

Date: _____

4th Monday of January

Date: _____

---

1 Samuel 17:47 New American Standard Bible (NASB)

[47] And that all this assembly may know that the LORD does not deliver by sword or by spear; for the battle is the LORD'S and He will give you into our hands."

John 21:6 New American Standard Bible (NASB)

[6] And He said to them, "Cast the net on the right- hand side of the boat and you will find a catch." So they cast, and then they were not able to haul it in because of the great number of fish.

Our prayer

Father God, we are facing difficult challenges in our lives today and we believe that you can save us because nothing is too difficult for you to do. It is impossible for us to find the right path without Your Divine intervention. We claim this promise that you can do the impossible for us in Jesus' name. Amen.

Talk to God:

_____

_____

What do the above verses mean to you?

1st Monday of January

Ecclesiastes 3:11

Meaning

Wait on God, He has good plans for you. In His perfect timing, He makes all thing beautiful for you and your circumstances, no matter how difficult it looks like right now.

2nd Monday of January

Isaiah 65:17

Meaning

God will bring you to a new life replacing the old one that was so full of confusion and living in sin. The glory of the new life would be such that the former ones would not be remembered. God do not make a record of them once forgiven.

3rd Monday of January

1 Samuel 17:47

Meaning

Who would think David would defeat Goliath? When God fights for you, your enemies will fall. God does not need your help in the battle, nor your tools and weaponry. He is God.

4th Monday of January

John 21:6

Meaning

Follow Jesus.
He said to Peter -- Cast the net on the right side of the ship. Peter hesitated then he changed his mind and obeyed Jesus. He caught so many fish that they could not pull the net back into the boat. This is a test of obedience. When you feel God telling to do something, obey Him and trust Him. God will bless you.

God Promises To Do The Impossible

1ˢᵗ Monday of February

Date: _____

> Hebrews 11:20 New
> American Standard Bible
> (NASB)
>
> [20] By faith Isaac blessed Jacob
> and Esau, even regarding
> things to come.

2ⁿᵈ Monday of February

Date: _____

> Hebrews 11:21 New
> American Standard Bible
> (NASB)
>
> [21] By faith Jacob, as he was
> dying, blessed each of the sons
> of Joseph, and worshiped,
> leaning on the top of his staff.

3ʳᵈ Monday of February

Date: _____

> Hebrews 11:22 New
> American Standard Bible
> (NASB)
>
> [22] By faith Joseph, when he was
> dying, made mention of the exodus
> of the sons of Israel, and gave
> orders concerning his bones

4ᵗʰ Monday of February

Date: _____

> Hebrews 11:23 New
> American Standard Bible
> (NASB)
>
> [23] By faith Moses, when he was
> born, was hidden for three months
> by his parents, because they saw
> he was a beautiful child; and they
> were not afraid of the king's edict.

Our prayer

Father God, we are facing difficult challenges in our lives today and we believe that you can save us because nothing is too difficult for you to do. It is impossible for us to find the right path without Your Divine intervention. We claim this promise that you can do the impossible for us in Jesus' name. Amen.

Talk to God:

_____

_____

What do the above verses mean to you?

1st Monday of February

> Hebrews 11:20
>
> Meaning
>
> Isaac who had strong faith was able to bless his two (2) sons Jacob first even if he was younger and then Esau. He believed that God will do great things with them. He cannot take away the blessing from Jacob. God allowed it, no one can take it away. Same thing with you. What you have from God, no one can take it from you. Pray for your children and guide them.

2nd Monday of February

> Hebrews 11:21
>
> Meaning
>
> Jacob's time was coming to an end; and he was able to bless his 2 grandchildren from Joseph, who he thought was dead long time ago. His faith proved he was right about Joseph and now Joseph's sons to pass the blessings. Let your generation of children know God. Bless them and pray for them.

3rd Monday of February

> Hebrews 11:22
>
> Meaning
>
> Joseph with strong faith, was able to see that the Israelites would leave Egypt one day and gave instructions about his bones. He wanted to go where his brothers would go. We all die, and make sure that you put thigs in order while you still can. Do not let your family fight over for your belongings.

4th Monday of February

> Hebrews 11:23
>
> Meaning
>
> Moses' life was spared by faith of his mother. She hid him for 3 months. God made a way for this baby to be raised like a prince. What would have been a tragedy became a great story. Never lose hope, when there seems to have no solution ahead and your enemies (illness, financial, people, difficulties etc.) look big & strong. God will never leave you. He will guide and protect you. You will have great testimonies of success ahead of you.

God Promises To Do The Impossible

1st Monday of March

Date: _____

2nd Monday of March

Date: _____

Hebrews 11:24 New American Standard Bible (NASB)

24 By faith Moses, when he had grown up, refused to be called the son of Pharaoh's daughter,

---

Hebrews 11:29 New American Standard Bible (NASB)

29 By faith they passed through the Red Sea as though they were passing through dry land; and the Egyptians, when they attempted it, were drowned.

3rd Monday of March

Date: _____

4th Monday of March

Date: _____

Hebrews 11:30 New American Standard Bible (NASB)

30 By faith the walls of Jericho fell down after they had been encircled for seven days.

Luke 1:37 New American Standard Bible (NASB)

37 For nothing will be impossible with God."

Our prayer

Father God, we are facing difficult challenges in our lives today and we believe that you can save us because nothing is too difficult for you to do. It is impossible for us to find the right path without Your Divine intervention. We claim this promise that you can do the impossible for us in Jesus' name. Amen.

Talk to God:

_____

_____

What do the above verses mean to you?

1st Monday of March

Hebrews 11:24

Meaning

Strong in faith, Moses knew he was saved by God when he was a baby, to do great things to his people, the Israelites. He refused to continue to live with false identity. Maybe you are not living right with God? Find out what does not belong to you and give them up. Be true to yourself and with God.

2nd Monday of March

Hebrews 11:29

Meaning

Parting of the Red Sea. Nothing is impossible with God, He saved his people from the Egyptians and made a way for them. Remember this verse when you are facing difficulties, He will part your "Red Sea" and you will walk thru it harmless.

3rd Monday of March

Hebrews 11:30

Meaning

Patience and obedience to God, the Israelites waited for 7 days to move in, they knew it was the right time appointed by God. They won the battle.

This is a conditional promise. Wait on God. Pray for wisdom & guidance.

4th Monday of March

Luke 1:37

Meaning

Believe in God without wavering. Trust Him. He can do all things. Even if you cannot see a solution and seems impossible. FOR NOT WITH GOD

God Promises To Do The Impossible

1st Monday of April

Date: _____

> Matthew 19:26 New American Standard Bible (NASB)
>
> 26 And looking at them Jesus said to them, "With people this is impossible, but with God all things are possible."

2nd Monday of April

Date: _____

> Genesis 1:1 New American Standard Bible (NASB
>
> The Creation
>
> 1 In the beginning God created the heavens and the earth.

3rd Monday of April

Date: _____

> Genesis 19:24 New American Standard Bible (NASB)
>
> 24 Then the Lord rained on Sodom and Gomorrah brimstone and fire from the Lord out of heaven,

4th Monday of April

Date: _____

> Exodus 3:3 New American Standard Bible (NASB)
>
> 3 So Moses said, must turn aside now and see this marvelous sight, why the bush is not burned up."

Our prayer

Father God, we are facing difficult challenges in our lives today and we believe that you can save us because nothing is too difficult for you to do. It is impossible for us to find the right path without Your Divine intervention. We claim this promise that you can do the impossible for us in Jesus' name. Amen.

Talk to God:

_____

_____

What do the above verses mean to you?

1st Monday of April

Matthew 19:26

Meaning

This is about a rich man who wants to be saved but walked away when Jesus told the rich man to sell everything he had and follow him. The rich man walked away and lose his salvation. No one can enter heaven except thru Jesus. He is the only way. Follow Jesus. We must call on Jesus because all things are possible with him.

2nd Monday of April

Genesis 1:1

Meaning

God was already there at beginning of time. He created the world. He is the creator of the universe. He created you He knows you.

3rd Monday of April

Genesis 19:24

Meaning

With warnings and signs, if people would not listen, God could destroy them just like Sodom and Gomorrah. Remember God is slow to anger, Go to Him and ask for forgiveness. He forgives.

4th Monday of April

Exodus 3:3

Meaning

This is when God called Moses to do something. God revealed Himself in a symbol of fire. Unapproachable Holiness. You notice that when God wants you to do something, you feel the heat inside you like a burning bush. That is God. Follow His promptings.

God Promises To Do The Impossible

1st Monday of May

Date: _____

Exodus 16:35 New American
Standard Bible
(NASB)

35 The sons of Israel ate the manna
forty years, until they came to
an inhabited land; they ate the
manna until they came to the
border of the land of Canaan.

2nd Monday of May

Date: _____

Exodus 17:6 New American
Standard Bible
(NASB)

6 Behold, I will stand before you
there on the rock at Horeb; and
you shall strike the rock, and water
will come out of it that the people
may drink." And Moses did so in
the sight of the elders of Israel.

3rd Monday of May

Date: _____

1 Kings 19:6 New American
Standard Bible
(NASB)

6 Then he looked and behold,
there was at his head a bread
cake baked on hot stones, and
a jar of water. So he ate and
drank and lay down again.

4th Monday of May

Date: _____

Acts 8:39 New American
Standard Bible (NASB)

39 When they came up out of
the water, the Spirit of the Lord
snatched Philip away; and the
eunuch no longer saw him, but
went on his way rejoicing.

Our prayer

Father God, we are facing difficult challenges in our lives today and we believe that
you can save us because nothing is too difficult for you to do. It is impossible for
us to find the right path without Your Divine intervention. We claim this promise
that you can do the impossible for us in Jesus' name. Amen.

Talk to God:

_____

_____

What do the above verses mean to you?

1st Monday of May

Exodus 16:35

Meaning

The manna must but eaten daily not be hoarded up. That was the condition. The Israelites did not follow this commandment but still God continued to provide for them for 40 years. That is how good God is. Another way of looking at this. Had they obeyed, it would have not taken 40 years to find the promised land. Obey God. Seek His wisdom, guidance and provision always.

2nd Monday of May

Exodus 17:6

Meaning

The children of Israel were thirsty and in need of drinking water. Moses pleaded to God and got instructions to strike the rock and water will flow. It did, in the sight of the elders of Israel.

When you meet troubles or lack that seems impossible to resolve, this is when our faith is tested. Call on God, He will meet your needs and that God may be glorified in your relief.

3rd Monday of May

1 Kings 19:6

Meaning

Elijah was fearful of Jezebel. He forgot how God fought for him and was scared of this woman. He ran and was desperate and hungry. An angel of the Lord brought him food.

At our most desperate time, we forget what God had done to us before, His goodness and mercy were always there. But we are blinded & afraid. We focus on the negative. Lift you head up to God, He will make a way for you. Do not doubt or be afraid of people. Just trust Him.

4th Monday of May

Acts 8:39

Meaning

Philip was snatched by Spirit of the Lord and placed him in another location. His purpose was already accomplished in the life of this Ethiopian.

God will send people in our lives to enlighten us. They may stay quickly but their message stays forever with you. Hold on to your faith.

God Promises To Do The Impossible

1st Monday of June

Date: _____

Matthew 14:21 New American Standard Bible (NASB) 21 There were about five thousand men who ate, besides women and children.

2nd Monday of June

Date: _____

Mark 6:44 New American Standard Bible (NASB) 44 There were five thousand men who ate the loaves.

3rd Monday of June

Date: _____

Luke 9:14-17 New American Standard Bible (NASB) 14(For there were about five thousand men.) And He said to His disciples, "Have them sit down to eat in groups of about fifty each." 15 They did so, and had them all sit down. 16 Then He took the five loaves and the two fish, and looking up to heaven, He blessed them, and broke them, and kept giving them to the disciples to set before the people. 17 And they all ate and were satisfied;

4th Monday of June

Date: _____

John 6:11 New American Standard Bible (NASB) 11 Jesus then took the loaves, and having given thanks, He distributed to those who were seated; likewise also of the fish as much as they wanted.

Our prayer

Father God, we are facing difficult challenges in our lives today and we believe that you can save us because nothing is too difficult for you to do. It is impossible for us to find the right path without Your Divine intervention. We claim this promise that you can do the impossible for us in Jesus' name. Amen.

Talk to God:

_____

_____

What do the above verses mean to you?

1st Monday of June

Matthew 14:21

Meaning

All 5000 men besides women and children were filled and satisfied. With twelve basketful left over of broken pieces. How great is that! God gives abundantly, exceedingly and overflowing. We have a gracious God. In this gospel, the people did not even ask for food, and yet Jesus knew they were hungry and he fed them. Follow Jesus.

2nd Monday of June

Mark 6:44

Meaning

Another version from Mark on the feeding of 5000 men. Coming only from five loaves of bread and 2 fish. Jesus commanded the people to sit down by groups on the green grass. Then he multiplied the 5 loaves and 2 fish in front of their eyes, they ate and all were satisfied. Whatever resources you have, offer them to Jesus. Organize your stuff. Share to those in need more than you. Our God is a God of order, not disorder. Do your best and God will do the rest. Trust Jesus.

3rd Monday of June

Luke 9:14-17

Meaning

This is Luke's version of the feeding of 5000. From 5 loaves of bread and 2 fish, Jesus look up to heaven and bless the food. He commanded to let the people sit down in groups of about fifty each group.

We reflect on the goodness of God and His provision. Somewhat a conditional promise. We have to order our lives first, ready yourself for increase. Then God will bless you more.

4th Monday of June

John 6:11

Meaning

Apostle John's version of the feeding of 5000. This gospel was written by the 4 of them: Matthew, Luke, Mark and John. Same message. Jesus fed the 5000 men, besides men and children. This can easily reach to double or even triple number of people to feed. Yet they were all satisfied. And 12 baskets of left-overs. From very little resources, just 5 loaves and 2 fish, miraculously multiplied beyond belief. Whatever little you have, don't discount them. Give them to God, He will increase them. Thank God always.

God Promises To Do The Impossible

1st Monday of July

Date: _____

> Mark 16:19 New American
> Standard Bible
> (NASB)
>
> 19 So then, when the Lord Jesus
> had spoken to them, He was
> received up into heaven and sat
> down at the right hand of God.

2nd Monday of July

Date: _____

> Genesis 1:2 New American
> Standard Bible
> (NASB)
>
> 2 The earth was formless and
> void, and darkness was over
> the surface of the deep, and the
> Spirit of God was moving over
> the surface of the waters.

3rd Monday of July

Date: _____

> Genesis 5:24 New American
> Standard Bible
> (NASB)
>
> 24 Enoch walked with God;
> and he was not, for
> God took him.

4th Monday of July

Date: _____

> Genesis 15:17 New American
> Standard Bible
> (NASB)
>
> 17 It came about when the sun had
> set, that it was very dark, and
> behold, there appeared a smoking
> oven and a flaming torch which
> passed between these pieces.

Our prayer

Father God, we are facing difficult challenges in our lives today and we believe that you can save us because nothing is too difficult for you to do. It is impossible for us to find the right path without Your Divine intervention. We claim this promise that you can do the impossible for us in Jesus' name. Amen.

Talk to God:

_____

_____

What do the above verses mean to you?

1st Monday of July

Mark 16:19

Meaning

This was the last time Jesus spoke to his disciples. He now sits at the right hand of the God the Father. He commissioned the eleven disciples to spread the good news.

When things are tough in life, remember that Jesus, our savior is there with the Father, who knows how you feel because he experienced pain and suffering while here on earth. He will ease your pain and give you hope. Call on Jesus.

2nd Monday of July

Genesis 1:2

Meaning

God created the world from formless void existence. There was confusion, emptiness and darkness. It was without beauty, order or even use. The Spirit of God was moving above the water, He separated the light from darkness. Nothing is too hard for God to do.

3rd Monday of July

Genesis 5:24

Meaning

It is possible for man not to die. Enoch was the first man without physical death. He was a man of God. Enoch lived for three hundred and sixty-five years before he was taken up to heaven. God took him.

God gives life and God takes life. It is all up to God when. We have our own appointed time. How & When? No one knows. Praise God always.

4th Monday of July

Genesis 15:17

Meaning

Abraham made his offerings to God in 2 sides. God accepted them. Signified by the burning torch that passed thru the sacrificed pieces in 2 sides. Fire symbolizes the presence of God.

Give your best offerings to God in a form obedience and worship & praises. God will be pleased with you.

God Promises To Do The Impossible

1st Monday of August

Date: _____

2nd Monday of August

Date: _____

Exodus 13:21 New American
Standard Bible
(NASB)

21 The LORD was going before
them in a pillar of cloud by day
to lead them on the way, and
in a pillar of fire by night to
give them light, that they might
travel by day and by night.

Exodus 14:29 New American
Standard Bible
(NASB)

29 But the sons of Israel walked
on dry land through the midst
of the sea, and the waters were
like a wall to them on their
right hand and on their left.

3rd Monday of August

Date: _____

4th Monday of August

Date: _____

Mark 15:33 New American
Standard Bible
(NASB)

33 When the sixth hour came,
darkness fell over the whole
land until the ninth hour

Exodus 40:35 New American
Standard Bible
(NASB)

35 Moses was not able to enter the
tent of meeting because the cloud
had settled on it, and the glory of
the LORD filled the tabernacle.

Our prayer

Father God, we are facing difficult challenges in our lives today and we believe that
you can save us because nothing is too difficult for you to do. It is impossible for
us to find the right path without Your Divine intervention. We claim this promise
that you can do the impossible for us in Jesus' name. Amen.

Talk to God:

_____

_____

What do the above verses mean to you?

1st Monday of August

> ## Exodus 13:21
>
> Meaning
>
> God led His people out of Egypt, in a pillar of fire by night to give them light, that they might travel by day and by night. Clouds by day. He gave them direction.
>
> In our difficulties and hardship in life, Let us ask Him for His guidance, that He gives us a clear direction, like a lamp in our paths.

2nd Monday of August

> ## Exodus 14:29
>
> Meaning
>
> Parting of the Red Sea. One of God's biggest miracle ever. No one can do this but God.
>
> When we encounter our Red Sea in life, pray on God. If He parted the sea for the Israelites, His children. He will remove that obstacle in front of you because you are His child too and He cares for you.

3rd Monday of August

> ## Mark 15:33
>
> Meaning
>
> When our Lord Jesus about to yield his spirit to the Father, there was darkness on earth, impossible to know the origin of this darkness. Clearly a supernatural event.
>
> When darkness comes to your life, hold to your faith because glory is about to happen. We cannot yet understand the plan of God at this time. We just have to trust in His will.

4th Monday of August

> ## Exodus 40:35
>
> Meaning
>
> The cloud was token of God's presence to the Israelites to be seen day and night. This is to encourage on this difficult journey.
>
> Just like in our own trials and difficulties, we seek God's presence in our cloudy path. God is our light, our God is a consuming fire. Keep your eyes on Jesus so you will not lose your way.

God Promises To Do The Impossible

1st Monday of September

Date: _____

2nd Monday of September

Date: _____

Leviticus 10:1 New American
Standard Bible
(NASB)

The Sin of Nadab and Abihu
[10] Now Nadab and Abihu, the sons
of Aaron, took their respective
firepans, and after putting fire
in them, placed incense on it and
offered strange fire before the LORD,
which He had not commanded them.

Numbers 11:1 New American
Standard Bible
(NASB)

The People Complain
[11] Now the people became like those
who complain of adversity in the
hearing of the LORD; and when
the LORD heard it, His anger was
kindled, and the fire of the LORD
burned among them and consumed
some of the outskirts of the camp.

3rd Monday of September

Date: _____

4th Monday of September

Date: _____

Mark 15:38 New American
Standard Bible
(NASB)

[38] And the veil of the temple was
torn in two from top to bottom.

Judges 6:21 New American
Standard Bible
(NASB)

[21] Then the angel of the LORD
put out the end of the staff that
was in his hand and touched the
meat and the unleavened bread;
and fire sprang up from the rock
and consumed the meat and the
unleavened bread. Then the angel of
the LORD vanished from his sight.

Our prayer

Father God, we are facing difficult challenges in our lives today and we believe that
you can save us because nothing is too difficult for you to do. It is impossible for
us to find the right path without Your Divine intervention. We claim this promise
that you can do the impossible for us in Jesus' name. Amen.

Talk to God:

_____

_____

What do the above verses mean to you?

1st Monday of September

Leviticus 10:1

Meaning

God commands respect.
Keep what is Holy, Holy.
In this case God acted
severely. Nadab and Abihu
were consumed by fire. Enter
in the place of God with
Humility and obedience.
Fear God. Love God.

2nd Monday of September

Numbers 11:1

Meaning

They complained and murmured
sinfully before the Lord God.
He heard them and angered
Him. The fire of the Lord burned
among them until Moses prayed
that the fire died down.

Praise and thank God
whatever your situation is.
He hears and knows your thoughts.
You can complain with pleading
not mocking Him. Remember
those days He blessed you.
God is here for you.

3rd Monday of September

Mark 15:38

Meaning

This temple was a holy place
for the Jews. There was the
beautiful thick, costly veil of
purple and gold veil which was
torn in two from top to bottom
when Jesus breathed his last.

God can go anywhere He wants
to go. Even on the temple of
people who crucified Jesus.
God can come to your
homes and bless you.
Open your hearts and
home for Him.
Thank you Jesus.

4th Monday of September

Judges 6:21

Meaning

Gideon, known to us now as a
great warrior was scared when
faced with a powerful enemy
he was about to fight. He made
food as offering to God to have
assurance that God will be with
him; and God consumed them
with fire to show His acceptance.
Fire signifies presence of God.

What are you going to offer God
when you need His presence during
difficult times? Do what is right,
show love & mercy to others. Praise
Him, Sing to Him. Honor God.

God Promises To Do The Impossible

1st Monday of October

Date: _____

2nd Monday of October

Date: _____

1 Kings 18:37-39 New American Standard Bible (NASB)

[37] Answer me, O LORD, answer me, that this people may know that You, O LORD, are God, and that You have turned their heart back again." [38] Then the fire of the LORD fell and consumed the burnt offering and the wood and the stones and the dust, and licked up the water that was in the trench. [39] When all the people saw it, they fell on their faces; and they said, "The LORD, He is God; the LORD, He is God."

2 Kings 2:8 New American Standard Bible (NASB)

[8] Elijah took his mantle and folded it together and struck the waters, and they were divided here and there, so that the two of them crossed over on dry ground.

3rd Monday of October

Date: _____

4th Monday of October

Date: _____

2 Kings 2:11 New American Standard Bible (NASB)

[11] As they were going along and talking, behold, there appeared a chariot of fire and horses of fire which separated the two of them. And Elijah went up by a whirlwind to heaven.

2 Kings 2:21-22 New American Standard Bible (NASB)

[21] He went out to the spring of water and threw salt in it and said, "Thus says the Lord, 'I have purified these waters; there shall not be from there death or unfruitfulness any longer.'" [22] So the waters have been [d] purified to this day, according to the word of Elisha which he spoke.

Our prayer

Father God, we are facing difficult challenges in our lives today and we believe that you can save us because nothing is too difficult for you to do. It is impossible for us to find the right path without Your Divine intervention. We claim this promise that you can do the impossible for us in Jesus' name. Amen.

Talk to God:

_____

_____

What do the above verses mean to you?

1ˢᵗ Monday of October

1 Kings 18:37-39

Meaning

Elijah was put on a trial by fire to prove that his God was the Most High God. There are other so-called prophets whose god was Baal. Elijah's prayer was heard. God consumed the burnt offering and licked the water that was on the trench. Only our God can do this. The other non-believers were punished by death. God will show up at the right time. Call on Him especially during your most challenging moments. He will not let his children be put to shame. He will save you from all your troubles. Praise God.

2ⁿᵈ Monday of October

2 Kings 2:8

Meaning

Another miracle of a parting of the water. This time at the Jordan. Then the 2 prophets walked thru dry land.

Nothing is impossible with God. According to His will and mercy, He can do impossible things for you. Trust God and you will walk on dry land too in the midst of the ocean of troubles.

3ʳᵈ Monday of October

2 Kings 2:11

Meaning

Another man who did not see death, was Elijah. Taken away by a chariot of Fire. Fire signifying God. Elijah's time on earth is over and God sent him a ride to heaven without tasting death.

When your life gets tough and seems hopeless look up to God and He can supernaturally lift you and take you away from that situation. Without knowing how you got out of the difficult situation, acknowledge Him. Thank God.

4ᵗʰ Monday of October

2 Kings 2:14

Meaning

The healing of the water. Elisha prayed and ask God to purify the drinking water and there will be no sickness, no death and unfruitfulness caused the by dirty water. God granted this request. In your life, ask God to purify you thru your challenges. Adversities and difficulties in life are the best purifier of our soul. Offer this to God. He will grant this request.

God Promises To Do The Impossible

1st Monday of November

Date: _____

> 2 Kings 6:6 New American
> Standard Bible
> (NASB)
>
> 6 Then the man of God said,
> "Where did it fall?" And when
> he showed him the place, he
> cut off a stick and threw it in
> there, and made the iron float.

2nd Monday of November

Date: _____

> 2 Kings 20:11 New American
> Standard Bible
> (NASB)
>
> 11 Isaiah the prophet cried to
> the LORD, and He brought the
> shadow on the stairway back
> ten steps by which it had gone
> down on the stairway of Ahaz.

3rd Monday of November

Date: _____

> Ezekiel 3:14 New American
> Standard Bible
> (NASB)
>
> 14 So the Spirit lifted me up
> and took me away; and I went
> embittered in the rage of my
> spirit, and the hand of the
> LORD was strong on me.

4th Monday of November

Date: _____

> Matthew 3:17 New American
> Standard Bible
> (NASB)
>
> 17 and behold, a voice out of the
> heavens said, "This is My beloved
> Son, in whom I am well- pleased."

Our prayer

Father God, we are facing difficult challenges in our lives today and we believe that you can save us because nothing is too difficult for you to do. It is impossible for us to find the right path without Your Divine intervention. We claim this promise that you can do the impossible for us in Jesus' name. Amen.

Talk to God:

_____

_____

What do the above verses mean to you?

1st Monday of November

2 Kings 6:6

Meaning

Just as when you fall,
God can pick you up.
You have to do your part too.
As Elisha said to lift up the iron,
God is telling you to get up
and do not be discouraged.
Find your way back up again.

2nd Monday of November

2 Kings 20:11

Meaning

God's confirmation of His
promise to extend the life of
Hezekiah. He made the shadow
to retreat 10 degrees. God
answered Hezekiah's prayer.

Call out to God just as the prophet
Isaiah did here. God can defy
nature to fulfill His promises to
you. Miracles still happens.

3rd Monday of November

Ezekiel 3:14

Meaning

When discouragement hits you and
you refuse to hear God's word, that
is pride. This can happen even to
righteous people. Pray for humility
and obedience. Only God is holy.

4th Monday of November

Matthew 3:17

Meaning

Jesus is the Son of God. He
is the Lord of Lords.
The Name above all Names.
Follow Jesus.

God Promises To Do The Impossible

1st Monday of December

Date: _____

2nd Monday of December

Date: _____

Matthew 14:25 New American Standard Bible (NASB)

25 And in the fourth watch of the night He came to them, walking on the sea.

Mark 6:48 New American Standard Bible (NASB)

48 Seeing them straining at the oars, for the wind was against them, at about the fourth watch of the night He *came to them, walking on the sea; and He intended to pass by them.

3rd Monday of December

Date: _____

4th Monday of December

Date: _____

Matthew 17:2 New American Standard Bible (NASB)

2 And He was transfigured before them; and His face shone like the sun, and His garments became as white as light.

Matthew 1:21 New American Standard Bible (NASB)

21 She will bear a Son; and you shall call His name Jesus, for He will save His people from their sins."

Our prayer

Father God, we are facing difficult challenges in our lives today and we believe that you can save us because nothing is too difficult for you to do. It is impossible for us to find the right path without Your Divine intervention. We claim this promise that you can do the impossible for us in Jesus' name. Amen.

Talk to God:

_____

_____

What do the above verses mean to you?

1st Monday of December

Matthew 14:25

Meaning

Who can walk in water?
Jesus did. The disciples
were terrified to see this.
Then Jesus calmed them down.
When fear overwhelms you, think
of this verse. How the disciples
must have felt when they saw
something they did not recognize
and coming near them. Then
there was Jesus who assures
them. Jesus will also say this to
Don't worry! I am Jesus.
Don't be afraid.

2nd Monday of December

Mark 6:48

Meaning

Another version of the story that
Jesus walked on the water. The
disciples were already struggling
against the wind when Jesus
came. Just as you struggle with so
many areas in your life, Jesus can
come in the middle of them and
calm the storms in your life. Do
not be terrified or be worried.
Jesus said. Don't worry! I am
Jesus. Don't be afraid.

3rd Monday of December

Matthew 17:2

Meaning

Jesus was with his three (3)
favorite disciples and he
showed his Divine side them.
He felt comfortable with them.
Jesus was transfigured.
His human face had a dazzling
glory upon it. Jesus is your friend.
Be comfortable with him. Tell Jesus
of your fears, worries, desires of
your heart. Talk to him daily.

4th Monday of December

Matthew 27:45

Meaning

The Birth of Jesus
Truly a miraculous birth and one of
the most important events during
that time. What a glorious day it
was! Why God did love us so much
to send Jesus to be among us? To
give us salvation and eternal life.
God cannot allow us to continue
to sin and will not spend eternity
with Him. Jesus was sent for
the forgiveness of our sins, to
show us the way. To show you
the way. Most of all to become
His children. You are a child
of the Most High God.
HE LOVES YOU!

Daily Guide – God Promises To Bless You Financially

Our Prayer

Father God, thank you for this promise of financial blessing.
Thank you, Lord, for paying our bills! Thank you for
showing us the way to go to live in prosperity, such as:
giving to the poor, obeying Your law and serving You.
And for anyone who has been given
much, much will be demanded.

Yes, let me be a happy giver.

We claim these promises believing you can
turn around our financial situation.

In the name of Jesus we pray. Amen

God Promises To Bless You Financially

1st Tuesday of January

Date: _____

2nd Tuesday of January

Date: _____

2 Chronicles 20:20 New American Standard Bible (NASB)
Enemies Destroy Themselves

20 They rose early in the morning and went out to the wilderness of Tekoa; and when they went out, Jehoshaphat stood and said, "Listen to me, O Judah and inhabitants of Jerusalem, put your trust in the Lord your God and you will be established. Put your trust in His prophets and succeed."

Deuteronomy 14:28 New American Standard Bible (NASB)

28"At the end of every third year you shall bring out all the tithe of your produce in that year, and shall deposit it in your town.

3rd Tuesday of January

Date: _____

4th Tuesday of January

Date: _____

Deuteronomy 16:17 New American Standard Bible (NASB)

17 Every man shall give as he is able, according to the blessing of the LORD your God which He has given you.

Psalm 126:6 New American Standard Bible (NASB)

6 He who goes to and fro weeping, carrying his bag of seed, Shall indeed come again with a shout of joy, bringing his sheaves with him.

Our prayer

Father God, thank you for this promise of financial blessing. Thank you Lord for paying our bills! Thank you for showing us the way to go to live in prosperity, such as: giving to the poor, obeying Your law and serving You. And from everyone who has been given much, much will be demanded. We claim this promise today in Jesus' name. Amen.

Talk to God:

_____

_____

What do the above verses mean to you?

1st Tuesday of January

2 Chronicles 20:20

Meaning

Rely on God if you desire
financial blessing.
Have courage, firmness of mind,
and be confident that God
is able to make His financial
promises manifest in your life,
including a victory over your
present financial challenges.

2nd Tuesday of January

Deuteronomy 14:28

Meaning

Your financial blessing is tied
to your ability to give to the
needy and the less privileged
around you. It is God's desire
that you have a feeling for those
who are in need including the
widow within your gates, and
the result of your obedient to
him is Financial BLESSING.
He will financially bless you
because you are obedient to Him!

3rd Tuesday of January

Deuteronomy 16:17

Meaning

How well are you giving from
the assets or abundance you have
experienced in the past? This
is a key to financial blessing!
This means if you want to be
blessed, you must give. Also,
you must not come or appear
before God with empty hands
to receive His blessing.
God loves a cheerful giver.

4th Tuesday of January

Psalm 126:6

Meaning

This is certainly a real-life event
that has spiritual lesson for you.
During the time for a farmer
to plant his seed, it is always a
season of hard work which can
literally cause so much stress.
You will do work and the result
of your hard work will definitely
pay off. You will need to endure
some tough times, which will
allow you appreciate God mercies
when He brings you through
those trials of life and gives
you victory over those trials.

God Promises To Bless You Financially

1st Tuesday of February

Date: _____

2nd Tuesday of February

Date: _____

Deuteronomy 28:1-2 New American Standard Bible (NASB)

Blessings at Gerizim

28 "Now it shall be, if you diligently obey the LORD your God, being careful to do all His commandments which I command you today, the LORD your God will set you high above all the nations of the earth. 2 All these blessings will come upon you and overtake you if you obey the LORD your God.

Deuteronomy 29:9 New American Standard Bible (NASB)

9 So keep the words of this covenant to do them, that you may prosper in all that you do.

3rd Tuesday of February

Date: _____

4th Tuesday of February

Date: _____

Deuteronomy 6:3 New American Standard Bible (NASB)

3 O Israel, you should listen and be careful to do it, that it may be well with you and that you may multiply greatly, just as the LORD, the God of your fathers, has promised you, in a land flowing with milk and honey.

Deuteronomy 8:18 New American Standard Bible (NASB)

18 But you shall remember the LORD your God, for it is He who is giving you power to make wealth that He may confirm His covenant which He swore to your fathers, as it is this day.

Our prayer

Father God, thank you for this promise of financial blessing. Thank you Lord for paying our bills! Thank you for showing us the way to go to live in prosperity, such as: giving to the poor, obeying Your law and serving You. And from everyone who has been given much, much will be demanded. We claim this promise today in Jesus' name. Amen.

Talk to God:

_____

_____

What do the above verses mean to you?

1st Tuesday of February

Deuteronomy 28:1-2

Meaning

This means to receive God's ultimate financial blessing, you need to submit yourself to the Lord your God and you will be financially blessed ultimately. Either in the form of prominence or financial prosperity. This implies that if you obey and keep all His commandment, He will pour you blessing irrespective of where you are. A conditional promise.

2nd Tuesday of February

Deuteronomy 29:9

Meaning

This follows the terms in the covenant"...and you will prosper in all you do..." Financial Prosperity comes as a result of your obedience to God. Meaning: faithfulness to God, which basically means observing the Word. Be prudent, act wisely, and you will be blessed. It is a blessing that comes from wise and prudent action that God commends you. A conditional promise.

3rd Tuesday of February

Deuteronomy 6:3

Meaning

God's blessing includes success in life, joy, peace of mind, a sense of fulfillment, and financial prosperity. All of these blessings are still available and obtainable if only you will hear and do it. And it is important to know also, that the blessing includes Wisdom, knowledge, direction, and understanding. A conditional promise.

4th Tuesday of February

Deuteronomy 8:18

Meaning

The Word of God is clear. We always need to remember that the Lord is the one who gives us the knowledge, ability, opportunity, and skill to be able to create wealth. Once we forget this, you cut yourself off the blessing God has promised you. A conditional promise.

God Promises To Bless You Financially

1st Tuesday of March

Date: _____

Ecclesiastes 5:18 New American Standard Bible (NASB)

18Here is what I have seen to be good and fitting: to eat, to drink and enjoy oneself in all one's labor which he toils under the sun during the few years of his life which God has given him; for this is his reward.

2nd Tuesday of March

Date: _____

Ecclesiastes 5:19-20 New American Standard Bible (NASB)

19Furthermore, as for every man to whom God has given riches and wealth, He has also empowered him to eat from them and to receive his reward and rejoice in his labor; this is the gift of God. 20 For he will not often consider the years of his life, because God keeps him occupied with the gladness of his heart.

3rd Tuesday of March

Date: _____

Genesis 14:18-20 New American Standard Bible (NASB)

18And Melchizedek king of Salem brought out bread and wine; now he was a priest of God Most High. 19He blessed him and said, "Blessed be Abram of God Most High, Possessor of heaven and earth; 20And blessed be God Most High, Who has delivered your enemies into your hand."

4th Tuesday of March

Date: _____

Genesis 26:12 New American Standard Bible (NASB)

12Now Isaac sowed in that land and reaped in the same year a hundredfold. And the Lord blessed him,

Our prayer

Father God, thank you for this promise of financial blessing. Thank you Lord for paying our bills! Thank you for showing us the way to go to live in prosperity, such as: giving to the poor, obeying Your law and serving You. And from everyone who has been given much, much will be demanded. We claim this promise today in Jesus' name. Amen.

Talk to God:

_____

_____

What do the above verses mean to you?

1st Tuesday of March

Ecclesiastes 5:18

Meaning

He encourages you to enjoy the fruit of your labor; eat, drink and enjoy the good life is the reason God bless you financially. A reward from God.

2nd Tuesday of March

Ecclesiastes 5:19-20

Meaning

The ability to enjoy life's financial stability is a "gift from God". In this passage, God uses Solomon to remind us that there are some gifts so valuable that they cannot be purchased with money – it is God's promise to His people to find fulfillment in your work by investing your riches for God's work and for His glory.

3rd Tuesday of March

Genesis 14:18-20

Meaning

God promised you a new understanding (new financial source), a bigger and better knowledge. God's purpose was to replace the old mentality (financial lack). Thank you Father God.

4th Tuesday of March

Genesis 26:12

Meaning
In the midst of famine and lack, you need to continually believe and look unto God and you will have it in abundance and run into financial overflow. Learn to do something that no one has ever tried to do. Sow in a land where nobody was sowing even in time famine! People may laugh at you as they watched you sow in a land that in the natural could not produce a harvest. You sowed because God promised to bless you regardless of the challenges in society. You have a promise already that if you sow a seed you will reap a harvest. Claim this promise.

God Promises To Bless You Financially

Date: _____

Date: _____

Isaiah 1:19 New American
Standard Bible
(NASB)

[19] "If you consent and obey, You
will eat the best of the land;

Isaiah 48:15 New American
Standard Bible
(NASB)

[15]"I, even I, have spoken;
indeed I have called him, I
have brought him, and He will
make his ways successful.

3rd Tuesday of April

Date: _____

4th Tuesday of April

Date: _____

Isaiah 48:17 New American
Standard Bible
(NASB)

[17]Thus says the LORD, your
Redeemer, the Holy One of Israel,
"I am the LORD your God, who
teaches you to profit, who leads
you in the way you should go.

Job 36:11 New American
Standard Bible (NASB)

[11]"If they hear and serve Him, They
will end their days in prosperity
And their years in pleasures.

Our prayer

Father God, thank you for this promise of financial blessing. Thank you Lord for paying our bills! Thank you for showing us the way to go to live in prosperity, such as: giving to the poor, obeying Your law and serving You. And from everyone who has been given much, much will be demanded. We claim this promise today in Jesus' name. Amen.

Talk to God:

_____

_____

What do the above verses mean to you?

1st Tuesday of April

Isaiah 1:19

Meaning

Your obedience means that you do not want to live a life of financial depravity, hardship, struggles, and strain. You follow Him. God withholds from those who doubt Him and rewards those who believe. If you want to be blessed you need to learn to walk in obedience. Isaac obeyed God and God blessed him right in the place where he was. God wants to do the same for you!

2nd Tuesday of April

Isaiah 48:15

Meaning

God has a plan for you, in which, for his own sake, and for the glory of His grace, He saves you as long as you are willing to come to Him. Claim this promise.

3rd Tuesday of April

Isaiah 48:17

Meaning

God wants to bless you greater than you have ever been blessed and He can do it if you are ready to be submissive. You don't have to go to another country, state, city, or neighborhood. He teaches you right where you are and turns everything around to profit you! Not only can He teaches you to profit, but it also leads you to where you should go. He can bless you in the midst of a suffering economy! Claim this promise.

4th Tuesday of April

Job 36:11

Meaning

Before the fall of man, the man was enjoying everything in abundance and God wants to restore you to that blessing. This he says according to God's promises. That is, if, as a result of your current challenges/afflictions, you repent, seek his God mercy, and serve him in time to come, you will prosper and enjoy prosperity and die in it. A conditional promise.

God Promises To Bless You Financially

1ˢᵗ Tuesday of May

Date: _____

Job 42:12 New American
Standard Bible
(NASB)

¹²The LORD blessed the latter days
of Job more than his beginning;
and he had 14,000 sheep and
6,000 camels and 1,000 yoke of
oxen and 1,000 female donkeys.

2ⁿᵈ Tuesday of May

Date: _____

Joshua 1:8 New American
Standard Bible
(NASB)

⁸This book of the law shall not
depart from your mouth, but
you shall meditate on it day and
night, so that you may be careful
to do according to all that is
written in it; for then you will
make your way prosperous, and
then you will have success.

3ʳᵈ Tuesday of May

Date: _____

Luke 10:7 New American
Standard Bible
(NASB)

⁷Stay in that house, eating and
drinking what they give you;
for the laborer is worthy of his
wages. Do not keep moving
from house to house.

4ᵗʰ Tuesday of May

Date: _____

Luke 12:31 New American
Standard Bible
(NASB)

³¹But seek His kingdom, and these
things will be added to you.

Our prayer

Father God, thank you for this promise of financial blessing. Thank you Lord for
paying our bills! Thank you for showing us the way to go to live in prosperity,
such as: giving to the poor, obeying Your law and serving You. And from everyone
who has been given much, much will be demanded. We claim this promise today
in Jesus' name. Amen.

Talk to God:

_____

_____

What do the above verses mean to you?

1st Tuesday of May

Job 42:12

Meaning

God's financial promises to us are to have it in abundance but you must always learn to trust Him. You need to relate to God primarily so that he will bless you with the stuff you want. The LORD blessed the latter part of Job's life more than the former part. Even if you are facing financial hardship now that you think it could prevent you from reaching your dream, this scripture encourages you to trust God more even though the situation is severe and more intense. We read that Job's latter life is blessed "more than his beginning". Claim this promise.

2nd Tuesday of May

Joshua 1:8

Meaning

God's great promise to you is I will be with you. This means much more than mere financial success, you need to constantly find out what God said concerning you and you know it through reading, and discoursing the word of God, and what shall come out of your mouth shall in all things be given according to His promise. A conditional promise. Say this: Yes Lord. I will!

3rd Tuesday of May

Luke 10:7

Meaning

Stay in God's plan, observe and do what He asks you to do; by keeping to His instruction then you will be worthy of his blessing. Do not keep moving from one to another, seeking for help where there is none. This also means be contented with what God you for now while He is still working on blessing you more. Thank you Lord.

4th Tuesday of May

Luke 12:31

Meaning

To seek the kingdom of God first is the fundamental choice you need to make as a follower of Jesus. Yet every day most people Christian life will either reinforce that decision or deny it. To enjoy God's blessing you will first need to put the things of God at your number one priority and then everything else you have ever desire will come to you.

God Promises To Bless You Financially

1st Tuesday of June

Date: _____

2nd Tuesday of June

Date: _____

Luke 12:34 New American Standard Bible (NASB)

34For where your treasure is, there your heart will be also.

Luke 6:38 New American Standard Bible (NASB)

38 Give, and it will be given to you. They will pour into your lap a good measure— pressed down, shaken together, and running over. For by your standard of measure it will be measured to you in return."

3rd Tuesday of June

Date: _____

4th Tuesday of June

Date: _____

Malachi 3:10 New American Standard Bible (NASB)

10 Bring the whole tithe into the storehouse, so that there may be food in My house, and test Me now in this," says the LORD of hosts, "if I will not open for you the windows of heaven and pour out for you a blessing until it overflows.

Mark 10:29-30 New American Standard Bible (NASB)

29Jesus said, "Truly I say to you, there is no one who has left house or brothers or sisters or mother or father or children or farms, for My sake and for the gospel's sake, 30but that he will receive a hundred times as much now in the present age, houses and brothers and sisters and mothers and children and farms, along with persecutions; and in the age to come, eternal life.

Our prayer

Father God, thank you for this promise of financial blessing. Thank you Lord for paying our bills! Thank you for showing us the way to go to live in prosperity, such as: giving to the poor, obeying Your law and serving You. And from everyone who has been given much, much will be demanded. We claim this promise today in Jesus' name. Amen.

Talk to God:

_____

_____

What do the above verses mean to you?

1st Tuesday of June

Luke 12:34

Meaning

You are a sheep of a great Shepherd, child of a great Father, and subjects of a great King. This Shepherd/King delights to financially bless you so that you also will be able to meet the financial need of others. What you treasure has massive implications on your blessing and security of our hearts. If you treasure giving, your receiving is secure. Thank you Father God.

2nd Tuesday of June

Luke 6:38

Meaning

This verse talks about how God wants to financially bless you, through which means, if you GIVE, you will RECEIVE. This principle is very clear and it relates to other bible verse: Whatever a man sows, that he will also reap. You will not only receive financially if you give but He will pour into your lap a good measure of financial abundance. Another conditional promise. Follow and claim this.

3rd Tuesday of June

Malachi 3:10

Meaning

If you obeyed God's commandment, you would be launched in the realm of financial rest. God desires to bless you financially if you will give generously to those in need, and especially to those who labor in the Word. I would encourage you to read Acts 4:31-35; 1 Corinthians 9:1-14; and 2 Corinthians 9:1-11 to see this principle. A conditional promise. Follow His command and be blessed!

4th Tuesday of June

Mark 10:29-30

Meaning

The reason He gave you this promise is to encourage you and help you make the right decisions even under threat. He clearly sets before you the promise of financial rewards if you will follow Him. God wants to build up your commitment to Him, He wants to bless you financially, and He wants you to have all sufficiently through the gospel. He wants you to look up and beyond to all that He has promised for those who faithfully follow Him.

God Promises To Bless You Financially

1st Tuesday of July

Date: _____

2nd Tuesday of July

Date: _____

Mark 4:8 New American
Standard Bible
(NASB)

8 Other seeds fell into the good soil,
and as they grew up and increased,
they yielded a crop and produced
thirty, sixty, and a hundredfold."

Matthew 5:42 New American
Standard Bible
(NASB)

42 Give to him who asks of you,
and do not turn away from him
who wants to borrow from you.

3rd Tuesday of July

Date: _____

4th Tuesday of July

Date: _____

Psalm 84:11 New American
Standard Bible
(NASB)

11 For the LORD God is a
sun and shield; The LORD
gives grace and glory;
No good thing does He
withhold from those
who walk upright.

Proverbs 10:2 New American
Standard Bible
(NASB)

2 Ill-gotten gains do not profit,
But righteousness
delivers from death.

Our prayer

Father God, thank you for this promise of financial blessing. Thank you Lord for paying our bills! Thank you for showing us the way to go to live in prosperity, such as: giving to the poor, obeying Your law and serving You. And from everyone who has been given much, much will be demanded. We claim this promise today in Jesus' name. Amen.

Talk to God:

_____

_____

What do the above verses mean to you?

1st Tuesday of July

Mark 4:8

Meaning

This Parable of the Sower tells you that your reception of God's Word is determined by the condition of your heart. This is because salvation is more than a superficial, if you are truly saved, you will go on to prove it. Your heart was moved by the Spirit to receive the Word when it was preached to you, as a result, your understandings were enlightened by it and you receive the comfortable experience of the truths of the word that come with power to you; it was a good word to you, and become good by the grace of God; the good work of grace was wrought upon your souls, and filled you with all financial blessings. Amen.

2nd Tuesday of July

Matthew 5:42

Meaning

Kindness of heart is a condition that God puts here to receive financial blessings. When your fellow Christians are in need, do not turn away from them. Do what you can to help and give them financial aid as well. Even if you know they cannot pay back, God will pay you for what you have given to them. Be kind and merciful is the condition that God telling you're here. Listen to Him and be blessed!

3rd Tuesday of July

Psalm 84:11

Meaning

Don't you want to have or drive a safe and reliable vehicle? Then control your emotion! Let the emotion motivate you. God wants to give you a financial blessing to live a better life, He wants to bless you in terms of finance but you must relax (do not worry or panic), you need to go to rest and allow Him to work because you can't be working while God is working. You either work and let God relax or you relax and let God be in charge.

4th Tuesday of July

Proverbs 10:2

Meaning

Crime does not pay and sin will not succeed, wickedness cannot profit but the blessing of the Lord makes you rich. No matter how much wealth you have accumulated through wickedness they are temporarily and will disappear within a short time. God cannot be bought off from judgment in this life or the next. Righteousness is the key to receive financial blessings from God successfully, and it will rescue you from several dangers.

God Promises To Bless You Financially

1st Tuesday of August

Date: _____

Proverbs 11:24-25 New
American Standard Bible
(NASB)

24 There is one who scatters, and
yet increases all the more,
And there is one who withholds
what is justly due, and yet
it results only in want.
25The generous man will be
prosperous, And he who waters
will himself be watered.

2nd Tuesday of August

Date: _____

Proverbs 11:16 New
American Standard Bible
(NASB)

16A gracious woman attains honor,
And ruthless men attain riches.

3rd Tuesday of August

Date: _____

Proverbs 12:24 New
American Standard Bible
(NASB)

24The hand of the diligent will rule,
But the slack hand will be
put to forced labor.

4th Tuesday of August

Date: _____

Proverbs 13:11 New
American Standard Bible
(NASB)

11Wealth obtained by
fraud dwindles,
But the one who gathers
by labor increases it.

Our prayer

Father God, thank you for this promise of financial blessing. Thank you Lord for paying our bills! Thank you for showing us the way to go to live in prosperity, such as: giving to the poor, obeying Your law and serving You. And from everyone who has been given much, much will be demanded. We claim this promise today in Jesus' name. Amen.

Talk to God:

_____

_____

What do the above verses mean to you?

1st Tuesday of August

Proverbs 11:24-25

Meaning

God will never bless a heart that never helps. This bible verse induce the fact that you should always make help at all times, if you don't sow, you won't reap, and if you don't give you will not receive. Therefore for you to have a success in financial status, you should always learn to help others. Through this, God will restore your finance at all time. To sum up: Give and you will receive.

2nd Tuesday of August

Proverbs 11:16

Meaning

Each gender has its own power. A woman by her beauty and character, wins favor. A man by his strength can gain riches, but may not win the favor of God. He has to have a heart to do good deeds, to obtain favor from the Lord's sight. Always strive to win the favor of God, and you will not lack provisions of all your needs. You be blessed!

3rd Tuesday of August

Proverbs 12:24

Meaning

Choose to be a diligent Christian and not a slothful one, this verse says, the hands of the diligent shall bear rule, but the slothful shall be under tribulations. Diligence matters a lot, always be a proactive Christian, a parable says an idle hand is a devil's workshop, God will never bless a slothful man, for you to receive the abundance of finances, you have to be diligent, once you choose to be one, of course, and God will be a supporter of you finances.

4th Tuesday of August

Proverbs 13:11

Meaning

This bible verse says wealth gotten by vanity shall be diminished: but he that gathers by labor shall increase. Therefore do not gather your wealth in an ungodly way whatsoever, fill your stomach with the labor of your hands. Our God is a merciful God, He will surely provide for you, and increase your portion in the circles of finances. When He sees your handwork, He will not leave you. Just keep a Godly heart, and gather your resources by the sweat of your eyebrows, God will increase you.

God Promises To Bless You Financially

1st Tuesday of September

Date: _____

| Proverbs 13:22 New American Standard Bible (NASB)

22 A good man leaves an inheritance to his children's children, And the wealth of the sinner is stored up for the righteous |

2nd Tuesday of September

Date: _____

| Proverbs 13:4 New American Standard Bible (NASB)

4The soul of the sluggard craves and gets nothing, But the soul of the diligent is made fat. |

3rd Tuesday of September

Date: _____

| Proverbs 14:23 New American Standard Bible (NASB)

23 In all labor there is profit, But mere talk leads only to poverty. |

4th Tuesday of September

Date: _____

| Proverbs 15:6 New American Standard Bible (NASB)

6Great wealth is in the house of the righteous, But trouble is in the income of the wicked. |

Our prayer

Father God, thank you for this promise of financial blessing. Thank you Lord for paying our bills! Thank you for showing us the way to go to live in prosperity, such as: giving to the poor, obeying Your law and serving You. And from everyone who has been given much, much will be demanded. We claim this promise today in Jesus' name. Amen.

Talk to God:

_____

_____

What do the above verses mean to you?

1ˢᵗ Tuesday of September

Proverbs 13:22

Meaning

The bible says a good name is rather to be chosen than great riches. Choose righteousness rather than silver and gold. Be a good example. A Godly example to others in terms of attitude, character, perception, and love would leave a good name and they will always speak positively for you. It can promote everything that concerns you all around and the riches of the unrighteous will fall into your hands. Follow God's law and Claim this promise.

2ⁿᵈ Tuesday of September

Proverbs 13:4

Meaning

This verse says the soul of the sluggard desires, and has nothing: but the soul of the diligent shall be made fat. Diligence with Faith is the key to riches, as God will only bless the work of your hands. Give something for God where He can bless you. If He doesn't find a good work in your hand He will not increase you, be diligent and you will surely receive from God.

3ʳᵈ Tuesday of September

Proverbs 14:23

Meaning

In all labor there is profit: but the talk of the lips without action produces nothing in return. What you do you for the Lord shall receive abundantly. If you labor you shall be blessed financially, and if you don't, it is also the other way round, I pray everything will turn around for your sake, and you will never end in need, Amen.

4ᵗʰ Tuesday of September

Proverbs 15:6

Meaning

Never pursue treasures and riches all day, a heart that forget God and pursue riches will not know peace. Give your heart to God. Fear Him and Love Him. You will be blessed abundantly both in material and heavenly things. While wickedness invites trouble in their lives. Follow God's commandments and you be blessed!

God Promises To Bless You Financially

1st Tuesday of October

Date: _____

Proverbs 17:8 New American
Standard Bible
(NASB)

8A bribe is a charm in the
sight of its owner; Wherever
he turns, he prospers.

2nd Tuesday of October

Date: _____

Proverbs 19:14 New
American Standard Bible
(NASB)

14House and wealth are an
inheritance from fathers, but a
prudent wife is from the LORD.

3rd Tuesday of October

Date: _____

Proverbs 19:17 New
American Standard Bible
(NASB)

17One who is gracious to a poor
man lends to the LORD,
And He will repay him
for his good deed.

4th Tuesday of October

Date: _____

Proverbs 21:5 New American
Standard Bible
(NASB)

5 The plans of the diligent
lead surely to advantage,
But everyone who is hasty
comes surely to poverty.

Our prayer

Father God, thank you for this promise of financial blessing. Thank you Lord for paying our bills! Thank you for showing us the way to go to live in prosperity, such as: giving to the poor, obeying Your law and serving You. And from everyone who has been given much, much will be demanded. We claim this promise today in Jesus' name. Amen.

Talk to God:

_____

_____

What do the above verses mean to you?

1st Tuesday of October

Proverbs 17:8

Meaning

A bribe is describe here like a gem, a precious stone; pleasant and acceptable, and dazzles the eyes. Tempting but not a nice thing to have if done with malice. Clean up those bad intentions like lusts, pride, and fakeness from your heart. You have earned the value of this precious gem. And you will prosper. A conditional promise.

2nd Tuesday of October

Proverbs 19:14

Meaning

House and riches are the inheritance of your earthly fathers: but a prudent wife can only come from the LORD. Everything good comes from God the Father, and to Him you should cast your burden and He will strengthen you, establish your finances and provide for your needs as well. God will also give something money cannot buy, a prudent wife / husband. Claim this promise.

3rd Tuesday of October

Proverbs 19:17

Meaning

He that has pity on the poor lends to the LORD; In everything you do, there is a reward, God sees your good deeds and He will surely anoints your finances for it to overflow. A conditional promise to be kind to the poor. Follow this command and claim this promise. You are blessed!

4th Tuesday of October

Proverbs 21:5

Meaning

It is important for you to know that as a Christian you need to strive for your purpose. When you are diligent with the talent God has given you, He will multiply the work of your hands and bless you as well, a lazy man will receive nothing, but God will always bless a diligent heart. Claim this promise.

God Promises To Bless You Financially

1st Tuesday of November

Date: _____

2nd Tuesday of November

Date: _____

> Proverbs 22:29 New
> American Standard Bible
> (NASB)
>
> 29Do you see a man
> skilled in his work?
> He will stand before kings;
> He will not stand before
> obscure men.

> Proverbs 22:4 New American
> Standard Bible
> (NASB)
>
> 4The reward of humility
> and the fear of the Lord
> Are riches, honor and life.

3rd Tuesday of November

Date: _____

4th Tuesday of November

Date: _____

> Proverbs 28:19-20 New
> American Standard
> Bible (NASB)
>
> 19 He who tills his land will
> have plenty of food, But he
> who follows empty pursuits
> will have poverty in plenty.
> 20 A faithful man will
> abound with blessings,
> But he who makes haste to be
> rich will not go unpunished.

> Proverbs 28:27 New
> American Standard Bible
> (NASB)
>
> 27He who gives to the poor will
> never want, But he who shuts his
> eyes will have many curses.

Our prayer

Father God, thank you for this promise of financial blessing. Thank you Lord for paying our bills! Thank you for showing us the way to go to live in prosperity, such as: giving to the poor, obeying Your law and serving You. And from everyone who has been given much, much will be demanded. We claim this promise today in Jesus' name. Amen.

Talk to God:

_____

_____

What do the above verses mean to you?

1st Tuesday of November

Proverbs 22:29

Meaning

With the skills that God gave you, offer them back to God. He will cause you to have Divine connections and you sit in high places. And earn the respect of your fellow Christian, along with distinctions and financial overflow. Claim this promise.

2nd Tuesday of November

Proverbs 22:4

Meaning

By humility and the fear of the LORD are riches, and honor in life. When you fear the lord, it's the beginning of wisdom, God will surely enlarge your coast and make you multiply in your finances, His provisions will never be outdated in your life, for His care for his children cannot be measured. Be humble. Claim this promise

3rd Tuesday of November

Proverbs 28:19-20

Meaning

The verse 28 says He who tills his land shall have plenty of bread: God will surely bless the work of your hands, this is a promise, and He will do it, He will do what He says, and He will make you flow in abundance of wealth. Thank you Father God.

4th Tuesday of November

Proverbs 28:27

Meaning

The bible verse says that he who gives to the poor shall not lack: but those who close their eyes and ignore the need of the poor, shall have many curses on them. You should know that God sees all your good deeds, and He will surely reward you abundantly in good measures, giving and helping others is a great way of showing love of God. He derives happiness from this because he Himself is love, and He will make sure He maintains your finances and provide your needs. Be generous and claim this promise.

God Promises To Bless You Financially

1st Tuesday of December

Date: _____

Proverbs 3:9-10 New American Standard Bible (NASB)

9 Honor the LORD from your wealth And from the first of all your produce;
10 So your barns will be filled with plenty And your vats will overflow with new wine.

2nd Tuesday of December

Date: _____

Proverbs 6:6-8 New American Standard Bible (NASB)

6 Go to the ant, O sluggard, Observe her ways and be wise,
7 Which, having no chief, Officer or ruler,
8 Prepares her food in the summer And gathers her provision in the harvest.

3rd Tuesday of December

Date: _____

Psalm 112:1-3 New American Standard Bible (NASB)

Prosperity of the One Who Fears the LORD.
112 Praise the LORD! How blessed is the man who fears the LORD, Who greatly delights in His commandments.
2 His descendants will be mighty on earth; The generation of the upright will be blessed.
3 Wealth and riches are in his house, And his righteousness endures forever.

4th Tuesday of December

Date: _____

Psalm 112:5 New American Standard Bible (NASB)

5 It is well with the man who is gracious and lends; He will maintain his cause in judgment.

Our prayer

Father God, thank you for this promise of financial blessing. Thank you Lord for paying our bills! Thank you for showing us the way to go to live in prosperity, such as: giving to the poor, obeying Your law and serving You. And from everyone who has been given much, much will be demanded. We claim this promise today in Jesus' name. Amen.

Talk to God:

_____

_____

What do the above verses mean to you?

1st Tuesday of December

2nd Tuesday of December

Proverbs 3:9-10

Meaning

Honor the LORD with your wealth,
and with the first fruits of all
your increases. By honoring God
with your wealth, He will surely
increase you, and when God
increases you, you are secured.
This is the same as the
principle of GOD FIRST.
And the rest God will take care.
Yes Lord. Amen.

Proverbs 6:6-8

Meaning

The ants work for their queen.
They carry food for her. Of course,
the queen takes care of them in
return. They have this kind of
obedience that is in their nature.
This verse is showing to be like
them in terms of obeying God.
Another angle is diligence. Be
diligence with your assignments
and prepare for the next season.
Be wise and do not be lazy. He
will multiply your output and
increase your finances. God wants
you to live a life of abundance.
Yes Lord. Amen.

3rd Tuesday of December

4th Tuesday of December

Psalm 112:1-3

Meaning

Blessed is the man who fears the
LORD and delights greatly in His
commandments, for God shall
multiply him and be put in a place
of excellence and leadership. For
many generations, wealth and
riches will stay with your family.
His blessings will stay with you
forever. Fear God. Love God.

Psalm 112:5

Meaning

When someone is in need and it
is within your means to help, you
have to lend a hand to that person,
accommodate and encourage him.
God will always guide your affairs
when you are of good deeds, He
will not let you down, He will
provide for your needs and He
will remove stagnancy from your
finances, He will enlarge you and
provide for all that you need.
Claim this promise.

Daily Guide – God Promises To Heal You

Our Prayer

Father God, thank you for this promise of healing. Your
words bring healing powers. They can ease our pain and
strengthen our bodies. Heal the illnesses our bodies. Heal
every kind of diseases in our bodies. Ease our pains. Heal our
love ones illnesses. Let there be no cancer cell in our bodies.

We claim these promises today believing
in your healing promises.

In the name of Jesus we pray. Amen

God Promises To Heal You

1st Wednesday of January

Date: _____

2nd Wednesday of January

Date: _____

Acts 4:10 New American
Standard Bible
(NASB)

¹⁰ let it be known to all of you and
to all the people of Israel, that
by the name of Jesus Christ the
Nazarene, whom you crucified,
whom God raised from the dead—
by this name this man stands
here before you in good health.

Isaiah 38:16 New American
Standard Bible
(NASB)

¹⁶ "O Lord, by these things
men live, And in all these is
the life of my spirit; O restore
me to health and let me live!

3rd Wednesday of January

Date: _____

4th Wednesday of January

Date: _____

Jeremiah 17:14 New
American Standard Bible
(NASB)

¹⁴ Heal me, O LORD, and I will be
healed; Save me and I will be saved,
For You are my praise.

John 6:63 New American
Standard Bible (NASB)

⁶³ It is the Spirit who gives life; the
flesh profits nothing; the words
that I have spoken to you are
spirit and are life.

Our prayer

Lord God, thank you for this promise of healing. Your words bring healing powers.
They can ease our pain and strengthen our bodies. We claim this promise today
in Jesus' name. Amen.

Talk to God:

_____

_____

What do the above verses mean to you?

1st Wednesday of January

Acts 4:10

Meaning

Jesus Christ of Nazarene who was crucified by men and God raised him from the dead. He bore our illnesses to give us healing and be of good health. Your healing is in the name of Jesus and no other for he has paid the price. Thank you Lord Jesus.

2nd Wednesday of January

Isaiah 38:16

Meaning

God can restore you back to health. Receive the spirit of God in your life and stay in agreement with His will. He is merciful. Discipline in lifestyle is an important to staying healthy. Follow this way of living and the Lord will restore your health and you will live well.

3rd Wednesday of January

Jeremiah 17:14

Meaning

When you make the Lord your praise; praising Him regularly, then you can ask Him to heal you, and you will be healed. Ask for forgiveness of sins and He will give you salvation. Pray in Jesus name. Amen.

4th Wednesday of January

John 6:63

Meaning

It is a choice to live in the spirit or by the flesh. The spirit thumps the flesh, in the order of things the flesh is earthly and causes us to sin. Put more importance on the Word of God to live by the Spirit. These Words that Lord has spoken to you is of the Spirit and it gives life. Claim this promise.

God Promises To Heal You

1st Wednesday of February

Date: _____

2nd Wednesday of February

Date: _____

Matthew 8:2-3 New
American Standard Bible
(NASB)

²And a leper came to Him and
bowed down before Him, and
said, "Lord, if You are willing,
You can make me clean."
³Jesus stretched out His hand and
touched him, saying, "I am willing;
be cleansed." And immediately
his leprosy was cleansed.

Proverbs 17:22 New
American Standard Bible
(NASB)

²²A joyful heart is good
medicine, But a broken
spirit dries up the bones.

3rd Wednesday of February

Date: _____

4th Wednesday of February

Date: _____

Proverbs 18:14 New
American Standard Bible
(NASB)

¹⁴The spirit of a man can endure
his sickness, But as for a broken
spirit who can bear it?

Psalm 107:20 New American
Standard Bible
(NASB)

²⁰He sent His word and healed
them, And delivered them
from their destructions.

Our prayer

Lord God, thank you for this promise of healing. Your words bring healing powers.
They can ease our pain and strengthen our bodies. We claim this promise today
in Jesus' name. Amen.

Talk to God:

_____

_____

What do the above verses mean to you?

1st Wednesday of February

Matthew 8:2-3

Meaning

The leper despised by everyone during that time was desperate for healing. With determination he approach Jesus to be healed. With humility he asked if Jesus is willing to heal him. Jesus said: I am willing. God is willing to heal you, reach out to him with a humble heart and He will heal you. Claim this promise.

2nd Wednesday of February

Proverbs 17:22

Meaning

Watch your heart. Guard it from darkness that will bring negativity in your thoughts. Sadness enhances sickness and brings death. A happy heart has a healing effect. Trust God and fill your heart with gladness. Healing will come with joyful heart. Thank you Lord.

3rd Wednesday of February

Proverbs 18:14

Meaning

Only the Holy Spirit can give you strength in heart and mind. This will affect your health as well. It is the spirit that keeps you going when you are weak, no one can stand a broken spirit. Endeavor to make your spirit strong always. Come Holy Spirit Come.

4th Wednesday of February

Psalm 107:20

Meaning

The word that the Lord sent will heal you and deliver you from discouragement. Keep His words and follow them. You will receive healing and encourages you to find hope and a future. Amen.

God Promises To Heal You

1st Wednesday of March

Date: _____

2nd Wednesday of March

Date: _____

Psalm 30:2 New American Standard Bible (NASB)

[2]O LORD my God,
I cried to You for help,
and You healed me.

---

1 Peter 2:24 New American Standard Bible (NASB)

[24]and He Himself bore our sins in His body on the cross, so that we might die to sin and live to righteousness; for by His wounds you were healed.

3rd Wednesday of March

Date: _____

4th Wednesday of March

Date: _____

---

1 Thessalonians 5:23 New American Standard Bible (NASB)

[23]Now may the God of peace Himself sanctify you entirely; and may your spirit and soul and body be preserved complete, without blame at the coming of our Lord Jesus Christ.

Acts 3:16 New American Standard Bible (NASB)

[16]And on the basis of faith in His name, it is the name of Jesus which has strengthened this man whom you see and know; and the faith which comes through Him has given him this perfect health in the presence of you all.

Our prayer

Lord God, thank you for this promise of healing. Your words bring healing powers. They can ease our pain and strengthen our bodies. We claim this promise today in Jesus' name. Amen.

Talk to God:

_____

_____

What do the above verses mean to you?

1st Wednesday of March

Psalm 30:2

Meaning

There is no other God like our God. We cry out to Him for our needs especially healing and He hears us. When you call on Him for whatever help you are in need of the Lord, He will send help in any form and shape, and also heal you. That is a given promise. God wants to heal you. Thank you Father God.

2nd Wednesday of March

1 Peter 2:24

Meaning

Jesus took your sins when he was crucified on the cross so that sin can be dead to you and now you live to righteousness. Now, by his wounds you are healed! Thank you Lord Jesus.

3rd Wednesday of March

1 Thessalonians 5:23

Meaning

The Lord will cleanse you of all impurities and make you holy. He will preserve your Spirit, soul and body against any attack, sin or any other impurity and you will be found holy without any sin on the judgement day. The Lord brings not only healing of body but also of the soul.

4th Wednesday of March

Acts 3:16

Meaning

Your healing depends on your faith. Do not doubt and believe in the Son of man. Through faith in the name of Jesus, you will be made strong and you will be completely healed. Thank you Lord Jesus.

God Promises To Heal You

1st Wednesday of April

Date: _____

2nd Wednesday of April

Date: _____

> Deuteronomy 7:15 New American Standard Bible (NASB)
>
> [15]The LORD will remove from you all sickness; and He will not put on you any of the harmful diseases of Egypt which you have known, but He will lay them on all who hate you.

> Psalm 34:10 New American Standard Bible (NASB)
>
> [10]The young lions do lack and suffer hunger; But they who seek the LORD shall not be in want of any good thing.

3rd Wednesday of April

Date: _____

4th Wednesday of April

Date: _____

> Deuteronomy 8:3 New American Standard Bible (NASB)
>
> [3]He humbled you and let you be hungry, and fed you with manna which you did not know, nor did your fathers know, that He might make you understand that man does not live by bread alone, but man lives by everything that proceeds out of the mouth of the LORD.

> Exodus 15:26 New American Standard Bible (NASB)
>
> [26]And He said, "If you will give earnest heed to the voice of the LORD your God, and do what is right in His sight, and give ear to His commandments, and keep all His statutes, I will put none of the diseases on you which I have put on the Egyptians; for I, the LORD, am your healer."

Our prayer

Lord God, thank you for this promise of healing. Your words bring healing powers. They can ease our pain and strengthen our bodies. We claim this promise today in Jesus' name. Amen.

Talk to God:

_____

_____

What do the above verses mean to you?

1st Wednesday of April

Deuteronomy 7:15

Meaning

People get sick now and then, that is normal. We serve a supernatural God, in this verse He said He will remove the sickness you have experienced or any harmful diseases, but rather He will cause your enemy to experience them. Claim this promise.

2nd Wednesday of April

Psalm 34:10

Meaning

Though this is more of provision and protection promise, it is here because hunger can make you ill. And also on the spiritual realm without food for the spirit, can make you sick both body and mind. Seek the Lord with all your hearts, you will not in want or lacking. Be blessed!

3rd Wednesday of April

Deuteronomy 8:3

Meaning

Then Lord will provide for you when you are hungry in way that you have never experienced before. Don't live by bread alone but by the word of God, because He is capable of providing for you and healing your illnesses. Be blessed!

4th Wednesday of April

Exodus 15:26

Meaning

If you listen to God and keep His commandments, no disease/ sickness will be able to come near you. A conditional promise. The condition is to earnestly listen and obey His word and He will heal your diseases. Does not mean you do not sin, but you do not live forever in sin. Ask for forgiveness. God is waiting for you. Keep calling on to God and follow Jesus.

God Promises To Heal You

1st Wednesday of May

Date: _____

> ### Psalm 34:19 New American Standard Bible (NASB)
>
> [19]Many are the afflictions of the righteous, But the LORD delivers him out of them all.

2nd Wednesday of May

Date: _____

> ### Exodus 23:2 New American Standard Bible (NASB)
>
> [2]You shall not follow the masses in doing evil, nor shall you testify in a dispute so as to turn aside after a multitude in order to pervert justice;

3rd Wednesday of May

Date: _____

> ### Exodus 23:25-26 New American Standard Bible (NASB)
>
> [25]But you shall serve the LORD your God, and He will bless your bread and your water; and I will remove sickness from your midst. [26] There shall be no one miscarrying or barren in your land; I will fulfill the number of your days.

4th Wednesday of May

Date: _____

> ### Galatians 3:29 New American Standard Bible (NASB)
>
> [29]And if you belong to Christ, then you are Abraham's descendants, heirs according to promise.

Our prayer

Lord God, thank you for this promise of healing. Your words bring healing powers. They can ease our pain and strengthen our bodies. We claim this promise today in Jesus' name. Amen.

Talk to God:

_____

_____

What do the above verses mean to you?

1st Wednesday of May

Psalm 34:19

Meaning

If you listen to voice of God and do good things, obeying His laid down rules and policies, then He will ensure that you will never suffer any sickness. Amen.

2nd Wednesday of May

Exodus 23:2

Meaning

You must be different in the midst of the crowd doing wrong things. When you are called to give your opinion, ensure you don't lie because of the people, always say the truth. Do not be a false witness. This is in the 10 Commandments too.

3rd Wednesday of May

Exodus 23:25-26

Meaning

It is important you serve God, if you do, He will provide for you and He will also protect you from sickness, there will be no issue with childbirth in your environment and He will give you long life. Another conditional promise. You shall serve the Lord. Claim this promise.

4th Wednesday of May

Galatians 3:29

Meaning

Now that you have given your life to Christ, you are child of Abraham, you are his heir and all God's promises to Abraham now belong to you also. Not by blood but by faith and accepting Jesus in your life. Amen.

God Promises To Heal You

1st Wednesday of June

Date: _____

Hosea 14:4 New American
Standard Bible
(NASB)

4I will heal their apostasy,
I will love them freely,
For My anger has turned
away from them.

2nd Wednesday of June

Date: _____

Isaiah 53:4-5 New American
Standard Bible
(NASB)

4 Surely our griefs He Himself
bore, And our sorrows He carried;
Yet we ourselves esteemed
Him stricken, Smitten of
God, and afflicted.
5 But He was pierced through
for our transgressions,
He was crushed for our iniquities;
The chastening for our well-
being fell upon Him, And by
His scourging we are healed.

3rd Wednesday of June

Date: _____

Isaiah 53:5 New American
Standard Bible
(NASB)

5But He was pierced through
for our transgressions,
He was crushed for our iniquities;
The chastening for our well-
being fell upon Him,
And by His scourging
we are healed.

4th Wednesday of June

Date: _____

Isaiah 58:11 New American
Standard Bible
(NASB)

11"And the LORD will continually
guide you, And satisfy your
desire in scorched places, And
give strength to your bones;
And you will be like a
watered garden,
And like a spring of water
whose waters do not fail.

Our prayer

Lord God, thank you for this promise of healing. Your words bring healing powers. They can ease our pain and strengthen our bodies. We claim this promise today in Jesus' name. Amen.

Talk to God:

_____

_____

What do the above verses mean to you?

1st Wednesday of June

Hosea 14:4

Meaning

A conditional promise to those who lost their way. God said RETURN to the Lord Your God. The Lord will forgive your sin, show you love without limits and all His anger towards you is gone. Call on Him and make Jesus your Lord and Savior. You are blessed!

2nd Wednesday of June

Isaiah 53:4

Meaning

God took your suffering on himself; He bore your pain. He bore your sorrow, was being punished for what you did. He was crushed because of your guilt. He took the punishment you deserved, and this brought you peace. You were healed because of His pain. God loves you. Claim this promise.

3rd Wednesday of June

Isaiah 53:5

Meaning

It was your sin He carried; it was your sorrow that weighed him down, but you thought your troubles were a punishment from God. But the opposite, God was beaten and battered for your own sins so that you could be whole again. . He was whipped, now you are healed. Thank God.

4th Wednesday of June

Isaiah 58:11

Meaning

The Lord will always lead you and meet your needs and re-energize you. You will flourish like well-tended garden, like an ever flowing spring. Praise God.

God Promises To Heal You

1st Wednesday of July

Date: _____

Isaiah 58:8 New American
Standard Bible
(NASB)

8"Then your light will break
out like the dawn, And your
recovery will speedily spring
forth; And your righteousness will
go before you; The glory of the
LORD will be your rear guard.

2nd Wednesday of July

Date: _____

Psalm 84:11 New American
Standard Bible
(NASB)

11For the LORD God is a
sun and shield; The LORD
gives grace and glory;
No good thing does He withhold
from those who walk uprightly.

3rd Wednesday of July

Date: _____

James 5:14-16 New American
Standard Bible
(NASB)

14Is anyone among you sick? Then
he must call for the elders of the
church and they are to pray over
him, anointing him with oil in the
name of the Lord; 15 and the prayer
offered in faith will restore the one
who is sick, and the Lord will raise
him up, and if he has committed
sins, they will be forgiven him.
16 Therefore, confess your sins
to one another, and pray for one
another so that you may be healed.
The effective prayer of a righteous
man can accomplish much.

4th Wednesday of July

Date: _____

Jeremiah 17:14 New American
Standard Bible
(NASB)

14Heal me, O LORD, and I will be
healed; Save me and I will be saved,
For You are my praise.

Our prayer

Lord God, thank you for this promise of healing. Your words bring healing powers.
They can ease our pain and strengthen our bodies. We claim this promise today
in Jesus' name. Amen.

Talk to God:

_____

_____

What do the above verses mean to you?

1st Wednesday of July

Isaiah 58:8

Meaning

Observances of fasting.
Prayer and fasting goes hand in
hand especially you need healing.
This will make God listen to
your woes and afflictions.
Your light will begin to shine
like the light of dawn. Then
your wounds will heal. Your
"Goodness" will precede you,
and the Glory of the Lord
shall be right behind you.
Amen.

2nd Wednesday of July

Psalm 84:11

Meaning

Look how good is God. He is
your sun to light your path
and shield from sickness. He
gives graces to those who goes
to Him and will not withhold
good things that belong to you.
Glory to you oh Mighty Lord!
Praises to you oh Father God.
Amen.

3rd Wednesday of July

James 5:14-16

Meaning

When you are sick, ask the elders of
the church to come and anoint you
in the name of the Lord and pray
for you, such a prayer offered in
faith will heal you. Ask forgiveness
and He will forgive you. Confess
to each other the wrong things
you have done. Then pray for each
other. Do this so that God can
heal you. The effective prayer of
a righteous man can accomplish
much. Amen.

4th Wednesday of July

Jeremiah 17:14

Meaning

Pray for the Lord to heal you,
surely you will be healed. Ask
the Lord save you and surely you
will be saved. Praise the Lord!

God Promises To Heal You

1st Wednesday of August

Date: _____

> **Psalm 41:3-4 New American Standard Bible (NASB)**
>
> ³The LORD will sustain him upon his sickbed; In his illness, You restore him to health. ⁴As for me, I said, "O LORD, be gracious to me; Heal my soul, for I have sinned against You."

2nd Wednesday of August

Date: _____

> **Jeremiah 30:17 New American Standard Bible (NASB)**
>
> ¹⁷'For I will restore you to health And I will heal you of your wounds,' declares the LORD, 'Because they have called you an outcast, saying: "It is Zion; no one cares for her."'

3rd Wednesday of August

Date: _____

> **Jeremiah 33:6 New American Standard Bible (NASB)**
>
> ⁶Behold, I will bring to it health and healing, and I will heal them; and I will reveal to them an abundance of peace and truth.

4th Wednesday of August

Date: _____

> **John 10:10 New American Standard Bible (NASB)**
>
> ¹⁰The thief comes only to steal and kill and destroy; I came that they may have life, and have it abundantly.

Our prayer

Lord God, thank you for this promise of healing. Your words bring healing powers. They can ease our pain and strengthen our bodies. We claim this promise today in Jesus' name. Amen.

Talk to God:

_____

_____

What do the above verses mean to you?

1st Wednesday of August

Psalm 41:3-4

Meaning

Because you have made the
Lord your praise, He shall heal
you and he will save you.
He is gracious to you and will hear
your prayers. Claim this promise.

2nd Wednesday of August

Jeremiah 30:17

Meaning

The Lord will restore your health
and heal your wounds. Do not feel
rejected, saying no one cares about
Christians. You are a child of the
Most High God. You are blessed!

3rd Wednesday of August

Jeremiah 33:6

Meaning

The Lord will heal you and give
you sound health. He will make
you enjoy peace and keep safe from
danger. Most of all, He will bring
healing and good health to you.
Praise God!

4th Wednesday of August

John 10:10

Meaning

A thief comes to steal, kill, and
destroy. The enemies meant
to harm you physically and
spiritually. But Jesus came to give
you life, a life that is complete
and good. You will be blessed
abundantly and overflowing
with good things and good
health. Thank you Lord Jesus.

God Promises To Heal You

1st Wednesday of September

Date: _____

2nd Wednesday of September

Date: _____

Malachi 4:2 New American
Standard Bible
(NASB)

2"But for you who fear My name,
the sun of righteousness will rise
with healing in its wings; and
you will go forth and skip about
like calves from the stall.

Psalm 147:3 New American
Standard Bible
(NASB)

3He heals the brokenhearted
And binds up their wounds.

3rd Wednesday of September

Date: _____

4th Wednesday of September

Date: _____

Matthew 19:2 New American
Standard Bible
(NASB)

2and large crowds followed Him,
and He healed them there.

Matthew 8:16 New American
Standard Bible
(NASB)

16When evening came, they
brought to Him many who were
demon-possessed; and He cast
out the spirits with a word,
and healed all who were ill.

Our prayer

Lord God, thank you for this promise of healing. Your words bring healing powers.
They can ease our pain and strengthen our bodies. We claim this promise today
in Jesus' name. Amen.

Talk to God:

_____

_____

What do the above verses mean to you?

1st Wednesday of September

Malachi 4:2

Meaning

For you that honor the Lord, the sun of righteousness will dawn on you with healing radiating from its wing. You will be free and happy, like captive that was let lose. Praise the Lord!

2nd Wednesday of September

Psalm 147:3

Meaning

Do not be brokenhearted for the Lord God cares for you and will heal you. Honor God and follow His decrees, He will also bind up your wounds physically, emotionally, mentally and spiritually. Praise God.

3rd Wednesday of September

Matthew 19:2

Meaning

The Lord healed ALL those that followed him. Not just a few but ALL. Those who were sick, lost, hungry, hopeless and helpless, because they followed the Lord Jesus. Do the same. Follow Jesus. Be blessed!

4th Wednesday of September

Matthew 8:16

Meaning

Bring to God any problem that you are having. Surrender all to God. He will heal you physically and spiritually, the word of God will cast them out and heal you of every sickness. Praise God.

God Promises To Heal You

1st Wednesday of October

Date: _____

2nd Wednesday of October

Date: _____

Matthew 8:2-3 New American Standard Bible (NASB)

2 And a leper came to Him and [a]bowed down before Him, and said, "Lord, if You are willing, You can make me clean." 3 Jesus stretched out His hand and touched him, saying, "I am willing; be cleansed." And immediately his leprosy was cleansed.

Matthew 8:8 New American Standard Bible (NASB)

8 But the centurion said, "Lord, I am not worthy for You to come under my roof, but just say the word, and my servant will be healed.

3rd Wednesday of October

Date: _____

4th Wednesday of October

Date: _____

Matthew 9:35 New American Standard Bible (NASB)

35Jesus was going through all the cities and villages, teaching in their synagogues and proclaiming the gospel of the kingdom, and healing every kind of disease and every kind of sickness.

Philippians 4:19 New American Standard Bible (NASB)

19And my God will supply all your needs according to His riches in glory in Christ Jesus.

Our prayer

Lord God, thank you for this promise of healing. Your words bring healing powers. They can ease our pain and strengthen our bodies. We claim this promise today in Jesus' name. Amen.

Talk to God:

_____

_____

What do the above verses mean to you?

1st Wednesday of October

Matthew 8:16-17

Meaning

Jesus is willing to heal you. This leper asked Jesus this question to show us all what is in Jesus' heart. He has compassion to those who need healing and have nowhere to go. Instantly this leper was healed because of his faith. Follow Jesus and claim his healing blessings to you. He is willing.

2nd Wednesday of October

Matthew 8:8

Meaning

The word is as potent as the presence of God Himself and it is capable of healing you of every sickness. Humility, faith and total surrender are qualities this centurion had and his servant received healing. Do the same. Be humble, stay in faith and surrender all to God. He heals you. Amen.

3rd Wednesday of October

Matthew 9:35

Meaning

Just as Jesus was going about in synagogues teaching and proclaiming the good news, the same word is available today, as potent as ever and will you of every kind of sickness and diseases. Approach with faith. You will receive healing. Amen.

4th Wednesday of October

Philippians 4:19

Meaning

God will freely supply your every need according to His riches in glory in Christ Jesus. Claim this promise.

God Promises To Heal You

1st Wednesday of November

Date: _____

2nd Wednesday of November

Date: _____

Proverbs 12:18 New
American Standard Bible
(NASB)

18There is one who speaks rashly
like the thrusts of a sword,
But the tongue of the
wise brings healing.

Proverbs 3:7-8 New
American Standard Bible
(NASB)

7Do not be wise in your own
eyes; Fear the LORD and
turn away from evil.
8 It will be healing to your body
And refreshment to your bones.

3rd Wednesday of November

Date: _____

4th Wednesday of November

Date: _____

Proverbs 4:20-22 New
American Standard
Bible (NASB)

20My son, give attention
to my words; Incline your
ear to my sayings.
21Do not let them depart
from your sight;
Keep them in the midst
of your heart.
22 For they are life to
those who find them
And health to all their body.

Psalm 103:2 New American
Standard Bible
(NASB)

2Bless the LORD, O my soul, And
forget none of His benefits;

Our prayer

Lord God, thank you for this promise of healing. Your words bring healing powers.
They can ease our pain and strengthen our bodies. We claim this promise today
in Jesus' name. Amen.

Talk to God:

_____

_____

What do the above verses mean to you?

1st Wednesday of November

Proverbs 12:18

Meaning

When you speak without thinking, and your words can cut like a knife. Be wise, and your words can heal. Just as you want others to do unto you. Be kind and merciful.

2nd Wednesday of November

Proverbs 3:7-8

Meaning

Do not trust in your own wisdom, but fear and respect the Lord and stay away from evil. This will bring refreshing sound health. Wisdom is the beginning of knowledge that only comes from God. Praise God

3rd Wednesday of November

Proverbs 4:20-22

Meaning

Listen to the word of God, hold them dearly in your heart and never stop thinking about them. They will bring good health and healings when you are sick. Praise God.

4th Wednesday of November

Psalm 103:2

Meaning

Let your soul praise the Lord and never forget how kind He is, remember all the good things He has done for you. Count your numerous blessings and thank God always.

God Promises To Heal You

1st Wednesday of December

Date: _____

Psalm 106:48 New American
Standard Bible
(NASB)

48 Blessed be the Lord, the God of
Israel, From everlasting even to
everlasting. And let all the people
say, "Amen." Praise the Lord!

2nd Wednesday of December

Date: _____

Psalm 105:37 New American
Standard Bible
(NASB)

37 Then He brought them
out with silver and gold,
And among His tribes there
was not one who stumbled.

3rd Wednesday of December

Date: _____

Isaiah 41:10 New American
Standard Bible
(NASB)

10 'Do not fear, for I am with you;
Do not anxiously look about
you, for I am your God.
I will strengthen you, surely I will
help you, Surely I will uphold you
with My righteous right hand.'

4th Wednesday of December

Date: _____

Deuteronomy 32:39 New American
Standard Bible (NASB)

39 'See now that I, I am He, And
there is no god besides Me;
It is I who put to death and
give life. I have wounded
and it is I who heal,
And there is no one who can
deliver from My hand.

Our prayer

Lord God, thank you for this promise of healing. Your words bring healing powers.
They can ease our pain and strengthen our bodies. We claim this promise today
in Jesus' name. Amen.

Talk to God:

_____

_____

What do the above verses mean to you?

1st Wednesday of December

Psalm 106:48

Meaning

Forever and ever, continually
praise the Lord! David wrote this
Psalm, a man after God's heart.
Be like David and continually
sing praises to God and glorify
His name. You be blessed with
good health, abundance and
most of all eternal life. Amen.

2nd Wednesday of December

Psalm 105:37

Meaning

He led you out of difficult
times, coming out of it with
load of blessings and none of
your belongings or family will
be missing. He will show you
the path to righteousness.
Praise God.

3rd Wednesday of December

Isaiah 41:10

Meaning

Do not worry and fearsome
because of your illness,
God is with you.
He holds you with His
righteous right hand. The
word of God will heal you.
God loves you. Praise Him.

4th Wednesday of December

Psalm 147:3

Meaning

There is only God. He is
the God of Abraham, Jacob,
Joseph, Moses and David.
The God the Father of
our Lord Jesus.
He created you from nothing.
He can put you to death or
heal you. Talk to Him heart to
heart. Ask for your healing.
He is good and merciful. He
will heal you. Trust Him.
Give Him praises.
Amen.

Daily Guide – God Promises To Protect You

Our Prayer

Father God, thank you for this promise of protection.
Even though sometimes trouble comes, with You on our
side we feel protected from those who meant to harm us
mentally, emotionally, spiritually and physically. We need
Your protection from evil manipulations especially on
the youth planning to do havoc, endangering many lives
and embarrassments to their families. We need protection
of our children from predators of all kinds. We need
protection in our schools, cities and the whole country.

We claim these promises of protection
with faith in our hearts.

In the name of Jesus we pray. Amen

God Promises To Protect You

1st Thursday of January

Date: _____

2nd Thursday of January

Date: _____

Ezekiel 34:28 New American
Standard Bible
(NASB)

28 They will no longer be a prey
to the nations, and the beasts of
the earth will not devour them;
but they will live securely, and
no one will make them afraid.

Isaiah 41:10 New American
Standard Bible
(NASB)

10 Do not fear, for I am with you;
Do not anxiously look about
you, for I am your God.
I will strengthen you, surely I will
help you, Surely I will uphold you
with My righteous right hand.'

3rd Thursday of January

Date: _____

4th Thursday of January

Date: _____

Proverbs 3:24 New American
Standard Bible
(NASB)

24 When you lie down, you will
not be afraid; When you lie
down, your sleep will be sweet.

Psalm 27:1 New American
Standard Bible
(NASB)

A Psalm of Fearless Trust in God.
A Psalm of David.
27 The LORD is my light and my
salvation; Whom shall I fear?
The LORD is the defense of my life;
Whom shall I dread?

Our prayer

Father God, thank you for this promise of protection. Even though sometimes
trouble comes, with you on our side we feel protected from those who meant to
harm us mentally, emotionally, spiritually and physically. We claim this promise
today in Jesus' name. Amen

Talk to God:

_____

_____

What do the above verses mean to you?

1st Thursday of January

Ezekiel 34:28

Meaning

You have the assurance that you will no longer be a victim of circumstance. Your safety is guaranteed no matter the adversity that pervades the land, therefore you have nothing to fear. Count on God to be on your side.

2nd Thursday of January

Isaiah 41:10

Meaning

You have nothing to be scared of simply because you believe in the one true God. The promises were made repeatedly simply to reassure and strengthen your fate and also encourage you to have the courage to withstand any challenge that comes your way.

3rd Thursday of January

Proverbs 3:24

Meaning

No more nightmare, no more troubled sleep, why? Because God replaced yours sorrows with joy everlasting. Peace and harmony shall be your lot based on your promise to me.

4th Thursday of January

Psalm 27:1

Meaning

You don't have any reason to be afraid of anybody since you're always under His protection. His shield and armor to destroy is strong enough and capable of destroying your enemies.

God Promises To Protect You

1st Thursday of February

Date: _____

Psalm 91:9, 10 New American Standard Bible (NASB)

9 For you have made the LORD, my refuge, Even the Most High, your dwelling place. 10 No evil will befall you, Nor will any plague come near your tent.

2nd Thursday of February

Date: _____

1 Corinthians 10:13 New American Standard Bible (NASB)

13 No temptation has overtaken you but such as is common to man; and God is faithful, who will not allow you to be tempted beyond what you are able, but with the temptation will provide the way of escape also, so that you will be able to endure it.

3rd Thursday of February

Date: _____

Proverbs 2:11 New American Standard Bible (NASB)

11 Discretion will guard you, Understanding will watch over you

4th Thursday of February

Date: _____

Psalm 4:6 New American Standard Bible (NASB)

6 Many are saying, "Who will show us any good?" Lift up the light of Your countenance upon us, O Lord!

Our prayer

Father God, thank you for this promise of protection. Even though sometimes trouble comes, with you on our side we feel protected from those who meant to harm us mentally, emotionally, spiritually and physically. We claim this promise today in Jesus' name. Amen

Talk to God:

_____

_____

What do the above verses mean to you?

1st Thursday of February

Psalm 91:9, 10

Meaning

As a reward for keeping faith in God almighty, and doing the things he admonished. You are assured of His protection and your entire household are free of any sickness, disease or any challenge that will be too much for you to handle. Claim this promise.

2nd Thursday of February

1 Corinthians 10:13

Meaning

God made it known that temptation will always come the way of mortals, however, He also made you to understand that no matter the sort of temptation that comes your way, you will always have the opportunity or avenue to overcome them. Therefore, there will be no room for you to dwell in any unhealthy situation for too long.

3rd Thursday of February

Proverbs 2:11

Meaning

Discretion shall preserve you, understanding shall keep you: If you are wise, you shall be careful to avoid all evil company and evil practices. When wisdom has dominion over you, then it not only fills the head, but enters into the heart, and will preserve, both against corruptions within and temptations without. Pray always.

4th Thursday of February

Psalm 4:6

Meaning

God is good and gives you protection. He will take away danger in your way Trust in Him.

God Promises To Protect You

1st Thursday of March

Date: _____

---

2 Chronicles 16:9 New American Standard Bible (NASB)

9 For the eyes of the LORD move to and fro throughout the earth that He may strongly support those whose heart is completely His. You have acted foolishly in this. Indeed, from now on you will surely have wars."

2nd Thursday of March

Date: _____

Psalm 91:9-10 New American Standard Bible (NASB)

9 For you have made the LORD, my refuge, Even the Most High, your dwelling place. 10 No evil will befall you, Nor will any plague come near your tent.

3rd Thursday of March

Date: _____

Psalm 92:8-9 New American Standard Bible (NASB)

8 But You, O LORD, are on high forever. 9 For, behold, Your enemies, O LORD, For, behold, Your enemies will perish; All who do iniquity will be scattered.

4th Thursday of March

Date: _____

---

2 Thessalonians 3:3 New American Standard Bible (NASB)

3 But the Lord is faithful, and He will strengthen and protect you from the evil one.

Our prayer

Father God, thank you for this promise of protection. Even though sometimes trouble comes, with you on our side we feel protected from those who meant to harm us mentally, emotionally, spiritually and physically. We claim this promise today in Jesus' name. Amen

Talk to God:

_____

_____

What do the above verses mean to you?

1st Thursday of March

2 Chronicles 16:9

Meaning

As the omnipresent and omniscient God, He is always there for those that put their trust in Him. To ensure that no harm comes their way while He will allow those lacking in sound judgement and goodwill to experience troubles and the uncertainty of life.

2nd Thursday of March

Psalm 91:9-10

Meaning

Almighty God has given you assurance that since you have put all your trust in Him, and have tried to live according to His dictates; He will never allow you to be a victimized in any way. Even in times of crises, He will make sure that you are safe and no harm shall come to you. Claim this promise.

3rd Thursday of March

Psalm 92:8-9

Meaning

For God Almighty has got an everlasting reputation of always being there for those that put their trust in Him. He will keep you safe. Because God lives eternally, and neither sleeps nor slumbers, He is always vigilant to ensure that everyone will receive their respective judgement accordingly. He will not spare evil doers and neither will He allow your enemies to succeed in their wicked plans, rather He will put them in disarray.

4th Thursday of March

2 Thessalonians 3:3

Meaning

The Lord is a faithful God, he shall establish you, and keep you from evil, you have nothing to fear, His protection is forever sure in your life. Thank you Lord Jesus!

God Promises To Protect You

1st Thursday of April

Date: _____

2 Timothy 4:17-18 New American Standard Bible (NASB)

17 But the Lord stood with me and strengthened me, so that through me the proclamation might be fully accomplished, and that all the Gentiles might hear; and I was rescued out of the lion's mouth. 18 The Lord will rescue me from every evil deed, and will bring me safely to His heavenly kingdom; to Him be the glory forever and ever. Amen.

2nd Thursday of April

Date: _____

Deuteronomy 28:7 New American Standard Bible (NASB)

7 "The LORD shall cause your enemies who rise up against you to be defeated before you; they will come out against you one way and will flee before you seven ways.

3rd Thursday of April

Date: _____

Deuteronomy 33:12 New American Standard Bible (NASB)

12 Of Benjamin he said,
"May the beloved of the LORD
dwell in security by Him,
Who shields him all the day,
And he dwells between
His shoulders."

4th Thursday of April

Date: _____

Psalm 91:9-10 New American Standard Bible (NASB)

9 For you have made the
LORD, my refuge,
Even the Most High,
your dwelling place.
10 No evil will befall you,
Nor will any plague
come near your tent.

Our prayer

Father God, thank you for this promise of protection. Even though sometimes trouble comes, with you on our side we feel protected from those who meant to harm us mentally, emotionally, spiritually and physically. We claim this promise today in Jesus' name. Amen

Talk to God:

_____

_____

What do the above verses mean to you?

1st Thursday of April

2 Timothy 4:17-18

Meaning

God has always stood by you, guiding and protecting you at all times against life threatening situations. He has always ensured that you are on the right path and that through Him, other unbelievers would come to terms with eternal salvation.

2nd Thursday of April

Deuteronomy 28:7

Meaning

The Lord promised to protect you from your adversaries. That no matter how formidable they may appear, He will bring confusion among them. His favor is on your side. Claim this promise.

3rd Thursday of April

Deuteronomy 33:12

Meaning

You are holding onto the promise He made to Benjamin, that He will always be there to protect God's children. To make sure that no harm comes your way by leaving you in the hands of His angels.

4th Thursday of April

Psalm 91:9-10

Meaning

Almighty God has given you assurance that since you have put all your trust in Him, and have tried to live according to His dictates; He will never allow you to be a victimized in any way. Even in times of crises, He will make sure that you are safe and no harm shall come to you.

God Promises To Protect You

1st Thursday of May

Date: _____

2nd Thursday of May

Date: _____

Exodus 23:22 New American
Standard Bible
(NASB)

22 But if you truly obey his voice
and do all that I say, then I will be
an enemy to your enemies and an
adversary to your adversaries.

Ezekiel 34:28 New American
Standard Bible
(NASB)

28 They will no longer be a prey
to the nations, and the beasts of
the earth will not devour them;
but they will live securely, and
no one will make them afraid.

3rd Thursday of May

Date: _____

4th Thursday of May

Date: _____

Ezra 9:8-9 New American
Standard Bible
(NASB)

8 But now for a brief moment grace
has been shown from the LORD our
God, to leave us an escaped remnant
and to give us a peg in His holy place,
that our God may enlighten our eyes
and grant us a little reviving in our
bondage. 9 For we are slaves; yet in our
bondage our God has not forsaken us,
but has extended loving kindness to
us in the sight of the kings of Persia, to
give us reviving to raise up the house
of our God, to restore its ruins and to
give us a wall in Judah and Jerusalem.

Isaiah 41:10 New American
Standard Bible
(NASB)

10 'Do not fear, for I am with you;
Do not anxiously look about
you, for I am your God.
I will strengthen you, surely I will
help you, Surely I will uphold you
with My righteous right hand.'

Our prayer

Father God, thank you for this promise of protection. Even though sometimes
trouble comes, with you on our side we feel protected from those who meant to
harm us mentally, emotionally, spiritually and physically. We claim this promise
today in Jesus' name. Amen

Talk to God:

_____

_____

What do the above verses mean to you?

1st Thursday of May

Exodus 23:22

Meaning

The Lord promised that if you can do His biddings, that he would not only fight your battles but will ensure that no harm comes your way.

2nd Thursday of May

Ezekiel 34:28

Meaning

The Lord made it clear that you will no longer be a victim to the wicked ones, rather you shall keep you safe and make me strong and confident. God will be there to help you.

3rd Thursday of May

Ezra 9:8-9

Meaning

Despite all your shortcomings, He always makes a way for you. He has given you a second chance to make amends, while equally giving you the strength to overcome your challenges irrespective of how daunting they may seem. He will not allow you to wallow in dejection, rather He will lift you above sin and sorrows. He is your strength.

4th Thursday of May

Isaiah 41:10

Meaning

God told you not to be afraid or dismayed over your current situation, for He will be there for you. To help you maintain a righteous life. Claim this promise.

God Promises To Protect You

1st Thursday of June

Date: _____

| Isaiah 43:1 New American Standard Bible (NASB)

Israel Redeemed

43 But now, thus says the LORD, your Creator, O Jacob, And He who formed you, O Israel, "Do not fear, for I have redeemed you; I have called you by name; you are Mine! |

2nd Thursday of June

Date: _____

Isaiah 43:2 New American Standard Bible (NASB)

Israel Redeemed

2 "When you pass through the waters, I will be with you; And through the rivers, they will not overflow you. When you walk through the fire, you will not be scorched, Nor will the flame burn you.

3rd Thursday of June

Date: _____

Deuteronomy 31:6 New American Standard Bible (NASB)

6 Be strong and courageous, do not be afraid or tremble at them, for the Lord your God is the one who goes with you. He will not fail you or forsake you."

4th Thursday of June

Date: _____

James 4:7 New American Standard Bible (NASB)

7 Submit therefore to God. Resist the devil and he will flee from you.

Our prayer

Father God, thank you for this promise of protection. Even though sometimes trouble comes, with you on our side we feel protected from those who meant to harm us mentally, emotionally, spiritually and physically. We claim this promise today in Jesus' name. Amen

Talk to God:

_____

_____

What do the above verses mean to you?

1st Thursday of June

2nd Thursday of June

Isaiah 43:1

Meaning

God admonished you to remain steadfast and not be afraid because He has redeemed you. And even when you face great obstacles, that He will be there to perform miracles that will ensure you remain safe at all times.

Isaiah 43:2

Meaning

God promised your safety and you should not be afraid because He is with you. And even when you face great and surmountable obstacles that He will be there to perform miracles that will ensure you remain safe at all times. Water will not overflow over you.

3rd Thursday of June

4th Thursday of June

Deuteronomy 31:6

Meaning

Cast your faith on God, do not fear. I tell you can move mountains, Our God is a mighty man in battle, when He goes out with you, who can dare face you?, He will surely protect you and guide you against your foes, His protection is forever sure all you need is to take courage and have faith in God. Fear God.

James 4:7

Meaning

He promised that when you live a Godly life, that you will be able to overcome any evil that comes your way. A conditional promise: You must resist the devil. Set your mind on God.

God Promises To Protect You

1st Thursday of July

Date: _____

Job 11:18-19 New American Standard Bible (NASB)

18 "Then you would trust, because there is hope; And you would look around and rest securely. 19 "You would lie down and none would disturb you, And many would entreat your favor.

2nd Thursday of July

Date: _____

Job 5:22 New American Standard Bible (NASB)

22 "You will laugh at violence and famine, And you will not be afraid of wild beasts.

3rd Thursday of July

Date: _____

Psalm 92:8-9 New American Standard Bible (NASB)

8 But You, O LORD, are on high forever. 9 For, behold, Your enemies, O LORD, For, behold, Your enemies will perish; All who do iniquity will be scattered.

4th Thursday of July

Date: _____

Joshua 1:5 New American Standard Bible (NASB)

5 No man will be able to stand before you all the days of your life. Just as I have been with Moses, I will be with you; I will not fail you or forsake you.

Our prayer

Father God, thank you for this promise of protection. Even though sometimes trouble comes, with you on our side we feel protected from those who meant to harm us mentally, emotionally, spiritually and physically. We claim this promise today in Jesus' name. Amen

Talk to God:

_____

_____

What do the above verses mean to you?

1st Thursday of July

Job 11:18-19

Meaning

This is His message assuring you of your safety at all times, including your day-to-day activities as well as at night, when you are sleeping. And even in your most vulnerable moments, no one would intimidate or harass you. Claim His promise of Protection.

2nd Thursday of July

Job 5:22

Meaning

During times of trouble and economic meltdown, I will be able to live above aboard without being afraid. Trust God's protection on you.

3rd Thursday of July

Psalm 92:8-9

Meaning

Jesus made it clear that those who believes in God would forever be under His protection, and God will never allow any harm to come upon them.

4th Thursday of July

Joshua 1:5

Meaning

He promised never to forsake you all through your earthly sojourn, and despite the challenges that may come your way, He will never abandon you. God loves you.

God Promises To Protect You

1st Thursday of August

Date: _____

2nd Thursday of August

Date: _____

Leviticus 25:18 New American Standard Bible (NASB)

18 'You shall thus observe My statutes and keep My judgments, so as to carry them out, that you may live securely on the land.

Proverbs 1:33 New American Standard Bible (NASB)

33 "But he who listens to me shall live securely And will be at ease from the dread of evil."

3rd Thursday of August

Date: _____

4th Thursday of August

Date: _____

1 Peter 3:13 New American Standard Bible (NASB)

13 Who is there to harm you if you prove zealous for what is good?

Proverbs 18:10 New American Standard Bible (NASB)

10 The name of the LORD is a strong tower; The righteous runs into it and is safe.

Our prayer

Father God, thank you for this promise of protection. Even though sometimes trouble comes, with you on our side we feel protected from those who meant to harm us mentally, emotionally, spiritually and physically. We claim this promise today in Jesus' name. Amen

Talk to God:

_____

_____

What do the above verses mean to you?

1st Thursday of August

2nd Thursday of August

Leviticus 25:18

Meaning

In this verse, God stated that
for as long as you abide by
His commandments, that
He would ensure that you
are safe at all times.
This is a conditional promise. Do
your part to benefit from this.

Proverbs 1:33

Meaning

Here, God made it clear that
anyone who believes in Him
would not entertain any feeling
of foreboding but will rather
have peace in abundance.
This is a conditional promise. Do
your part to benefit from this.

3rd Thursday of August

4th Thursday of August

1 Peter 3:13

Meaning

The Lord assured you of full
protection provided you follow His
path and always do what is right.

Trust God.

Proverbs 18:10

Meaning

Righteous people would always
be protected by serving God.
They will find solace in His
name even in times of crises.
Claim this promise.

God Promises To Protect You

1st Thursday of September

Date: _____

2nd Thursday of September

Date: _____

Proverbs 3:24 New American
Standard Bible
(NASB)

24 When you lie down, you will
not be afraid; When you lie
down, your sleep will be sweet.

Proverbs 30:5 New American
Standard Bible
(NASB)

5 Every word of God is tested;
He is a shield to those who
take refuge in Him.

3rd Thursday of September

Date: _____

4th Thursday of September

Date: _____

Psalm 112:7 New American
Standard Bible
(NASB)

7 He will not fear evil tidings;
His heart is steadfast,
trusting in the LORD.

Psalm 4:8 New American
Standard Bible (NASB)

8 In peace I will both lie down and
sleep, For You alone, O LORD,
make me to dwell in safety.

Our prayer

Father God, thank you for this promise of protection. Even though sometimes trouble comes, with you on our side we feel protected from those who meant to harm us mentally, emotionally, spiritually and physically. We claim this promise today in Jesus' name. Amen

Talk to God:

_____

_____

What do the above verses mean to you?

1st Thursday of September

Proverbs 3:24

Meaning

God assured you that you shall have nothing to worry about, and even when you go to bed, you will be able to enjoy peaceful sleep. Thank you Father God.

2nd Thursday of September

Proverbs 30:5

Meaning

God is not a man that can revoke on His promise, rather He abides by His words and would always protect those that call upon Him. Amen.

3rd Thursday of September

Psalm 112:7

Meaning

The Lord told you not to be afraid of any unsavory situation, therefore you will put all your trust in Him alone. Yes Lord. Amen.

4th Thursday of September

Psalm 4:8

Meaning

This bible verse says you will lay down and sleep. The LORD God will make you dwell in safety. In tranquility of mind, resting securely upon God's promises, and the conduct of His wise and gracious providence, assures you not to be weary or afraid of little things, put your faith in God and He will intercede for you always.

God Promises To Protect You

1st Thursday of October

Date: _____

Psalm 121:3-8 New American
Standard Bible
(NASB)

3 He will not allow your foot to slip;
He who keeps you will not slumber.
4 Behold, He who keeps Israel
Will neither slumber nor sleep.
5 The LORD is your keeper;
The LORD is your shade
on your right hand.
6 The sun will not smite you by
day, Nor the moon by night.

2nd Thursday of October

Date: _____

Psalm 121:7 New American
Standard Bible
(NASB)

7 The LORD will protect you from
all evil; He will keep your soul.

3rd Thursday of October

Date: _____

John 1:5 New American
Standard Bible (NASB)

5 The Light shines in the darkness, and
the darkness did not comprehend it.

4th Thursday of October

Date: _____

Psalm 124:1-5 New American
Standard Bible (NASB)

124 "Had it not been the LORD who
was on our side," Let Israel now say,
2 "Had it not been the LORD
who was on our side
When men rose up against us,
3 Then they would have swallowed
us alive, When their anger
was kindled against us;
4 Then the waters would have
engulfed us, The stream would
have swept over our soul;
5 Then the raging waters would
have swept over our soul."

Our prayer

Father God, thank you for this promise of protection. Even though sometimes trouble comes, with you on our side we feel protected from those who meant to harm us mentally, emotionally, spiritually and physically. We claim this promise today in Jesus' name. Amen

Talk to God:

_____

_____

43-19

What do the above verses mean to you?

1st Thursday of October

2nd Thursday of October

Psalm 121:3-8

Meaning

For God is always awake, He will never allow you to be tormented. God is always focused and able to provide for your needs. He is always there to protect you from your adversaries. He will ensure that you are protected from your enemies; including those you are aware of and those that may come in disguise.

Psalm 121:7

Meaning

The Lord shall keep you safe from your enemies, He will ensure that you are well protected at all times. Claim this promise.

3rd Thursday of October

4th Thursday of October

John 1:5

Meaning

Where is darkness at the sight of light? Where is death when God has conquered it? Jesus is the light, and he will shine for you in the dark, he will ease your ways and protect you from all dangers, his protection is forever sure over your life. Thank you Lord Jesus.

Psalm 124:1-5

Meaning

What could you have done if God has not been on your side? Even when your enemies rose up against you, wishing that misfortune shall befall you, but God has remained with you, protecting you from harm. In all their attempts to make you suffer, God remained your refuge and at the end, he gave you peace everlasting.

God Promises To Protect You

1st Thursday of November

Date: _____

Psalm 18:2 New American
Standard Bible
(NASB)

2 The LORD is my rock and my
fortress and my deliverer,
My God, my rock, in whom I take
refuge; My shield and the horn
of my salvation, my stronghold.

2nd Thursday of November

Date: _____

Psalm 34:7 New American
Standard Bible
(NASB)

7 The angel of the LORD
encamps around those who
fear Him, And rescues them.

3rd Thursday of November

Date: _____

Psalm 4:8 New American
Standard Bible
(NASB)

8 In peace I will both lie down and
sleep, For You alone, O LORD,
make me to dwell in safety.

4th Thursday of November

Date: _____

Psalm 5:11 New American
Standard Bible
(NASB)

11 But let all who take refuge in You
be glad, Let them ever sing for joy;
And may You shelter them,
That those who love Your
name may exult in You.

Our prayer

Father God, thank you for this promise of protection. Even though sometimes trouble comes, with you on our side we feel protected from those who meant to harm us mentally, emotionally, spiritually and physically. We claim this promise today in Jesus' name. Amen

Talk to God:

_____

_____

43-21

What do the above verses mean to you?

1st Thursday of November

Psalm 18:2

Meaning

The Lord promised to always be there for you; to guild and protect you, provide for you and give you the strength to carry on. As you have put all your trust in Him, you should now take pride in the things of the Lord. Thank you Father God.

2nd Thursday of November

Psalm 34:7

Meaning

You should no longer harbour any fear whatsoever simply because God has given charge to His angels to always protect you at all times and also ensure that all your needs are met accordingly. Amen.

3rd Thursday of November

Psalm 4:8

Meaning

Your safety is assured by the Most High God, therefore, you have nothing to fear about during your going out and coming in, and when you go to bed, you will be able to sleep like a baby because you know your redeemer lives. Thank you Lord Jesus.

4th Thursday of November

Psalm 5:11

Meaning

When you put your trust in God, He will defend you in all circumstances and in Him you will always rejoice. When you put your trust in God He will never let you down, and of course His divine protection will be showered on you.

God Promises To Protect You

1st Thursday of December

Date: _____

Psalm 56:9 New American
Standard Bible
(NASB)

9 Then my enemies will turn
back in the day when I call;
This I know, that God is for me.

2nd Thursday of December

Date: _____

Psalm 57:1 New American
Standard Bible
(NASB)

Prayer for Rescue from Persecutors.
For the choir director; set to Al-
tashheth. A Mikhtam of David,
when he fled from Saul in the cave.
57 Be gracious to me, O God,
be gracious to me,
For my soul takes refuge in You;
And in the shadow of Your
wings I will take refuge Until
destruction passes by.

3rd Thursday of December

Date: _____

Psalm 61:3 New American
Standard Bible
(NASB)

3 For You have been a refuge for me,
A tower of strength
against the enemy.

4th Thursday of December

Date: _____

Psalm 91:3-5 New American
Standard Bible
(NASB)

3 For it is He who delivers you
from the snare of the trapper And
from the deadly pestilence.
4 He will cover you with His pinions,
And under His wings you may
seek refuge; His faithfulness
is a shield and bulwark.
5 You will not be afraid of the terror by
night, Or of the arrow that flies by day;

Our prayer

Father God, thank you for this promise of protection. Even though sometimes
trouble comes, with you on our side we feel protected from those who meant to
harm us mentally, emotionally, spiritually and physically. We claim this promise
today in Jesus' name. Amen

Talk to God:

_____

_____

What do the above verses mean to you?

1st Thursday of December

Psalm 56:9

Meaning

Whenever you're troubled and you call upon Him, he will always come to your rescue and put your oppressors to shame. He is always faithful to those that put their trust in Him.

2nd Thursday of December

Psalm 57:1

Meaning

In times of crises, you can look up to Him. For you have put all your trust in Him and have confidence in His ability to see you through during hard times such as this. He will not count on your iniquities but will always show mercy on you. Because He loves you.

3rd Thursday of December

Psalm 61:3

Meaning

God have always protected you in times of danger, against unforeseen circumstances. He will give you strength. Therefore, have faith that He will fight your battles. Thank you Lord Jesus.

4th Thursday of December

Psalm 91:3-5

Meaning

The Lord will ensure you are protected from deceivers of this world and also during crises. No matter how many attacks come against you in different shapes and forms, on any day and time, God promises to protect you always. He is bigger than your enemies. Count on Him.

Daily Guide – God Promises To Bring You Blessings

Our Prayer

When we proclaim the goodness of the Lord,
abundant grace will fall upon us.

We love You Lord! We magnify You
Lord! We praise You Lord!

You are the King of Kings! You are the Lord of Lords!

You are the name above all names!

We glorify You Lord! Alleluia! Alleluia! Alleluia!

We claim these promises of blessings
today believing in your goodness.

In the name of Jesus we pray. Amen

God Promises To Bring You Blessings

1st Friday of January

Date: _____

1 Peter 1:2 New American Standard Bible (NASB) 2 according to the foreknowledge of God the Father, by the sanctifying work of the Spirit, to obey Jesus Christ and be sprinkled with His blood: May grace and peace be yours in the fullest measure.

2nd Friday of January

Date: _____

1 Peter 3:9 New American Standard Bible (NASB) 9 not returning evil for evil or insult for insult, but giving a blessing instead; for you were called for the very purpose that you might inherit a blessing.

3rd Friday of January

Date: _____

2 Corinthians 1:2 New American Standard Bible (NASB) 2 Grace to you and peace from God our Father and the Lord Jesus Christ.

4th Friday of January

Date: _____

2 Corinthians 13:14 New American Standard Bible (NASB) 14 The grace of the Lord Jesus Christ, and the love of God, and the fellowship of the Holy Spirit, be with you all.

Our prayer

When we proclaim the goodness of the Lord, abundant grace will fall upon us. Yes Lord! You are the King of Kings! You are the Lord of Lords! You are the name above all names! We claim this promise of blessings today in Jesus name. Amen.

Talk to God:

_____

_____

What do the above verses mean to you?

1st Friday of January

1 Peter 1:2

Meaning

If you live by these words you will find peace, focus in life, good health and you will have financial stability. God will not forsake you. Do what is right/righteous and just, in accordance with the spirit and not society's standards, then you will enjoy the grace of God's provision which means just enough of everything you will require in life. You will also have peace and will be an inspiration to others.

2nd Friday of January

1 Peter 3:9

Meaning

This will help you control your anger and you will come off as a bigger person in heated situations. You will be more mature in thinking and actions, you will be a peace maker, you will be an inspiration to others and these values will open doors in aspects of your life, be it financial, academic or in your career.

3rd Friday of January

2 Corinthians 1:2

Meaning

This speaks of grace which signifies just enough of God's provision in all aspects of your life and peace which is a satisfaction that even money cannot buy will be yours and this will come from God the Father and God the Son. This will teach you how to be contented with what you have, you might not be very rich but you will be satisfied with the provisions God will give you.

4th Friday of January

2 Corinthians 13:14

Meaning

Pray for others, because no man is an island. You never know where your financial break through will come from. Fellowshipping is like networking, you get to meet different people and hopefully they will add value to your spiritual, emotional, financial and intellectual life.

God Promises To Bring You Blessings

1st Friday of February

Date: _____

2nd Friday of February

Date: _____

---

2 Samuel 13:25 New American Standard Bible (NASB)

25 But the king said to Absalom, "No, my son, we should not all go, for we will be burdensome to you." Although he urged him, he would not go, but blessed him.

---

2 Samuel 19:39 New American Standard Bible (NASB)

39 All the people crossed over the Jordan and the king crossed too. The king then kissed Barzillai and blessed him, and he returned to his place.

3rd Friday of February

Date: _____

4th Friday of February

Date: _____

---

2 Samuel 7:29 New American Standard Bible (NASB)

29 Now therefore, may it please You to bless the house of Your servant, that it may continue forever before You. For You, O Lord GOD, have spoken; and with Your blessing may the house of Your servant be blessed forever."

Acts 15:33 New American Standard Bible (NASB)

33 After they had spent time there, they were sent away from the brethren in peace to those who had sent them out.

Our prayer

When we proclaim the goodness of the Lord, abundant grace will fall upon us. Yes Lord! You are the King of Kings! You are the Lord of Lords! You are the name above all names! We claim this promise of blessings today in Jesus name. Amen.

Talk to God:

_____

_____

What do the above verses mean to you?

1st Friday of February

2 Samuel 13:25

Meaning

This speaks about when you are not on the same page with someone, or when you have a difference of opinion on a matter. You should not let it dissuade me, because you have been called to a higher anointing with the fear of God and the love you have in you. You must support and encourage anyone you have a difference of opinion with.

2nd Friday of February

2 Samuel 19:39

Meaning

Barzillai was a wealthy man that took care of David when he was at Mahanaim and because of that he found favor in the eyes of King David. He was eighty years old when David tried to reward Him but he charged David to pay it forward. My good deeds will find favor in the sight of great people.

When you are in the position to help the weak, poor, afflicted and destitute please do because you never know who they will become tomorrow.

3rd Friday of February

2 Samuel 7:29

Meaning

It is believed that the greatest accomplishment a Christian can have is hearing the voice of God. This verse speaks of a prayer for blessing because of a covenant made with God and this sacred agreement no matter what can never be broken by God. The prayer is made with humility and ambition, but without asking for anything in particular.

4th Friday of February

Acts 15:33

Meaning

This is a prayer shared between a group of people during times of trials and tribulations. It is a prayer of strength to face times of adversity and trouble. It is as easy as saying "Peace be unto you".
You might get scared and think that God has forsaken in times of trouble but hold on to your faith and trust in God. Bad things happens to everybody, it is how you deal with it that counts. Remember it is always darkest before the dawn.

God Promises To Bring You Blessings

1st Friday of March

Date: _____

2nd Friday of March

Date: _____

Deuteronomy 11:26 New American Standard Bible (NASB)

26 "See, I am setting before you today a blessing and a curse:

Deuteronomy 11:27 New American Standard Bible (NASB)

27 the blessing, if you listen to the commandments of the LORD your God, which I am commanding you today;

3rd Friday of March

Date: _____

4th Friday of March

Date: _____

Deuteronomy 12:15 New American Standard Bible (NASB)

15 "However, you may slaughter and eat meat within any of your gates, whatever you desire, according to the blessing of the LORD your God which He has given you; the unclean and the clean may eat of it, as of the gazelle and the deer.

Deuteronomy 23:5 New American Standard Bible (NASB)

5 Nevertheless, the LORD your God was not willing to listen to Balaam, but the LORD your God turned the curse into a blessing for you because the LORD your God loves you.

Our prayer

When we proclaim the goodness of the Lord, abundant grace will fall upon us. Yes Lord! You are the King of Kings! You are the Lord of Lords! You are the name above all names! We claim this promise of blessings today in Jesus name. Amen.

Talk to God:

_____

_____

What do the above verses mean to you?

1st Friday of March

Deuteronomy 11:26

Meaning

This is an explanation of the difference between a blessing and curse. On one hand a blessing comes from obedience and following the commandments of God which is made easy by the teachings and life of Jesus Christ. It means if you follow the Life and teachings of Jesus Christ you will receive blessings.

2nd Friday of March

Deuteronomy 11:27

Meaning

A conditional promise. If you follow God and live by His word, You will be blessed. Financial blessings, spiritual blessings, and success are yours. Praise God!

3rd Friday of March

Deuteronomy 12:15

Meaning

This speaks about the blessing God gives you and the instructions on how you should use them. God has given everyone one blessing or another to do his works and fulfill His righteousness and not your will and you must use these blessings in accordance to His will and plans. Pursue your passion, do not let anyone tell you that you cannot. God has put in you something special, do not be afraid of it, embrace it. It will change your financial situation.

4th Friday of March

Deuteronomy 23:5

Meaning

This is a prayer for when your enemies afflict, fight and curse you in the sight of God. Your Persecutors will claim that they are justified in cursing you but because of your steadfastness, good works and faith you have in the Lord, he will not forsake you or hand you over to your enemies. People will laugh at you and kick you when you are down and that it was all your fault and that you deserve what you get. Do not worry, pick yourself up, trust in God He will change your situation and put your detractors to shame.

God Promises To Bring You Blessings

1st Friday of April

Date: _____

> Deuteronomy 28:8 New American Standard Bible (NASB)
>
> 8 The LORD will command the blessing upon you in your barns and in all that you put your hand to, and He will bless you in the land which the LORD your God gives you.

2nd Friday of April

Date: _____

> Deuteronomy 29:19 New American Standard Bible (NASB)
>
> 19 It shall be when he hears the words of this curse that he will boast, saying, 'I have peace though I walk in the stubbornness of my heart in order to destroy the watered land with the dry.'

3rd Friday of April

Date: _____

> Deuteronomy 33:1 New American Standard Bible (NASB)
>
> The Blessing of Moses
>
> 33 Now this is the blessing with which Moses the man of God blessed the sons of Israel before his death.

4th Friday of April

Date: _____

> Deuteronomy 33:23 New American Standard Bible (NASB)
>
> 23 Of Naphtali he said, "O Naphtali, satisfied with favor, And full of the blessing of the LORD, Take possession of the sea and the south."

Our prayer

When we proclaim the goodness of the Lord, abundant grace will fall upon us. Yes Lord! You are the King of Kings! You are the Lord of Lords! You are the name above all names! We claim this promise of blessings today in Jesus name. Amen.

Talk to God:

_____

_____

What do the above verses mean to you?

1st Friday of April

Deuteronomy 28:8

Meaning

As a Christian that follows and lives by the word of God your hand work will not only be successful but anything you involve in or any where you are will be blessed and successful also, even in a wilderness, desert or barren land you will find favor from the Lord.

2nd Friday of April

Deuteronomy 29:19

Meaning

It means when you who is a believer strays from the word of God and his teachings and does not repent of it. You will not only destroy that which has been built but also that which is to come. You will not only bring ruin to yourself but to others as well.

3rd Friday of April

Deuteronomy 33:1

Meaning

This is a prayer of Love and good fortune from one who has been ordained by God.

4th Friday of April

Deuteronomy 33:23

Meaning

When you keep the commandment and follow the instructions of the Lord, You will gain favor in the sight of others and the blessings of God will show in your life through your accomplishments and achievements.

God Promises To Bring You Blessings

1st Friday of May

Date: _____

2nd Friday of May

Date: _____

Ephesians 4:29 New
American Standard Bible
(NASB)

29 Let no unwholesome word
proceed from your mouth, but
only such a word as is good for
edification according to the need
of the moment, so that it will
give grace to those who hear.

Exodus 23:25 New American
Standard Bible
(NASB)

25 But you shall serve the LORD
your God, and He will bless your
bread and your water; and I will
remove sickness from your midst.

3rd Friday of May

Date: _____

4th Friday of May

Date: _____

Ezekiel 34:26 New American
Standard Bible
(NASB)

26 I will make them and the
places around My hill a blessing.
And I will cause showers to
come down in their season; they
will be showers of blessing.

Ezekiel 44:30 New American
Standard Bible
(NASB)

30 The first of all the first
fruits of every kind and every
contribution of every kind,
from all your contributions,
shall be for the priests; you
shall also give to the priest the
first of your dough to cause a
blessing to rest on your house.

Our prayer

When we proclaim the goodness of the Lord, abundant grace will fall upon us.
Yes Lord! You are the King of Kings! You are the Lord of Lords! You are the name
above all names! We claim this promise of blessings today in Jesus name. Amen.

Talk to God:

_____

_____

What do the above verses mean to you?

1st Friday of May

Ephesians 4:29

Meaning

You should not profane or demoralize people. First you listen before you speak in-order to tailor you response to the particular individual. If God has given you charge to speak to people, you must use it to uplift their spirit.

2nd Friday of May

Exodus 23:25

Meaning

When you serve God in spirit and in truth, whatever it is that you gather or that is a part of you will be blessed. Your body and mind will be free of illness and everyone around me will be sanctified as well.

3rd Friday of May

Ezekiel 34:26

Meaning

This is the blessing of the promises of God on you and the land you dwell in.

4th Friday of May

Ezekiel 44:30

Meaning

If you are anointed by God to do his works, or chosen to guide his flock, those who show you favor will also find favor in the sight of the Lord.

God Promises To Bring You Blessings

1st Friday of June

Date: _____

2nd Friday of June

Date: _____

Genesis 12:2 New American Standard Bible (NASB)

2 And I will make you a great nation, And I will bless you, And make your name great; And so you shall be a blessing;

Genesis 2:17 New American Standard Bible (NASB)

17 but from the tree of the knowledge of good and evil you shall not eat, for in the day that you eat from it you will surely die."

3rd Friday of June

Date: _____

4th Friday of June

Date: _____

Genesis 27:10 New American Standard Bible (NASB)

10 Then you shall bring it to your father that he may eat, so that he may bless you before his death."

Genesis 27:12 New American Standard Bible (NASB)

12 Perhaps my father will feel me, then I will be as a deceiver in his sight, and I will bring upon myself a curse and not a blessing."

Our prayer

When we proclaim the goodness of the Lord, abundant grace will fall upon us. Yes Lord! You are the King of Kings! You are the Lord of Lords! You are the name above all names! We claim this promise of blessings today in Jesus name. Amen.

Talk to God:

_____

_____

What do the above verses mean to you?

1st Friday of June

Genesis 12:2

Meaning

This is from a covenant with God and the promises thereof. If you find favor in the sight of God he will not only make you grow in all aspects, but he will make you to be remembered and you will be a blessing to others.

2nd Friday of June

Genesis 2:17

Meaning

This is a warning of what not to do. The tree here signifies consciousness and out of that comes imagination and out of that desire and out of that sin and that leads to death.

3rd Friday of June

Genesis 27:10

Meaning

This is a blessing that can be passed from one generation to another it comes from the covenant made with God that is binding and forever.

4th Friday of June

Genesis 27:12

Meaning

This is a comment made by Jacob and indeed he was cursed and he and his generation suffered many afflictions but because he was redeemed and blessed under the name of Israel his father's covenant with God was never broken.

God Promises To Bring You Blessings

1st Friday of July
Date: _____

2nd Friday of July
Date: _____

Genesis 27:19 New American
Standard Bible
(NASB)

19 Jacob said to his father, "I am Esau your firstborn; I have done as you told me. Get up, please, sit and eat of my game, that you may bless me."

Genesis 27:25 New American
Standard Bible
(NASB)

25 So he said, "Bring it to me, and I will eat of my son's game, that I may bless you." And he brought it to him, and he ate; he also brought him wine and he drank.

3rd Friday of July
Date: _____

4th Friday of July
Date: _____

Genesis 27:4 New American
Standard Bible
(NASB)

4 and prepare a savory dish for me such as I love, and bring it to me that I may eat, so that my soul may bless you before I die."

Genesis 28:4 New American
Standard Bible
(NASB)

4 May He also give you the blessing of Abraham, to you and to your descendants with you, that you may possess the land of your sojourning, which God gave to Abraham."

Our prayer

When we proclaim the goodness of the Lord, abundant grace will fall upon us. Yes Lord! You are the King of Kings! You are the Lord of Lords! You are the name above all names! We claim this promise of blessings today in Jesus name. Amen.

Talk to God:

_____

_____

What do the above verses mean to you?

1st Friday of July

> ### Genesis 27:19
>
> ### Meaning
>
> This is the generational blessing. This is one instance when Jacob deceived his father Isaac. Jacob is not the first born but Esau. Not an ideal situation to follow. But sometimes God is telling us to be bold to receive your blessings.

2nd Friday of July

> ### Genesis 27:25
>
> ### Meaning
>
> The game which is made into a meal and presented as an offering is like a ritual to get the favor of the father. If he finds the offering pleasing, he will pass on the blessing. It shows the power that comes from giving.

3rd Friday of July

> ### Genesis 27:4
>
> ### Meaning
>
> This talks about following instructions in order to receive the generational blessing.

4th Friday of July

> ### Genesis 28:4
>
> ### Meaning
>
> This speaks of the promises of God, how it grows from generation to generation and how the blessing not only falls upon you but around where ever you are in terms of your Location.

God Promises To Bring You Blessings

1st Friday of August

Date: _____

Genesis 39:5 New American
Standard Bible
(NASB)

5 It came about that from the
time he made him overseer in
his house and over all that he
owned, the LORD blessed the
Egyptian's house on account of
Joseph; thus the LORD'S blessing
was upon all that he owned, in
the house and in the field.

2nd Friday of August

Date: _____

Hebrews 6:7 New American
Standard Bible
(NASB)

7 For ground that drinks the rain
which often falls on it and brings
forth vegetation useful to those
for whose sake it is also tilled,
receives a blessing from God;

3rd Friday of August

Date: _____

Isaiah 19:24 New American
Standard Bible
(NASB)

24 In that day Israel will be the third
party with Egypt and Assyria, a
blessing in the midst of the earth,

4th Friday of August

Date: _____

Isaiah 44:3 New American
Standard Bible
(NASB)

3 'For I will pour out water
on the thirsty land
And streams on the dry ground;
I will pour out My Spirit
on your offspring
And My blessing on
your descendants;

Our prayer

When we proclaim the goodness of the Lord, abundant grace will fall upon us.
Yes Lord! You are the King of Kings! You are the Lord of Lords! You are the name
above all names! We claim this promise of blessings today in Jesus name. Amen.

Talk to God:

_____

_____

What do the above verses mean to you?

1ˢᵗ Friday of August

Genesis 39:5

Meaning

This speaks of the generational blessing. Jacob who later turned to Israel married two sisters but the second which was the wife he intended to marry initially had two sons and the anointing of the Lord was upon the first child Joseph, even at an early age, and this made his elder brothers despise Him. Where ever he went and whatever he did the favor and promises of the Lord was with Him.

2ⁿᵈ Friday of August

Hebrews 6:7

Meaning

This talks about nature and following the rules of nature according to how God intended. When we respect nature and live in balance with it we will in turn receive blessing from god.

3ʳᵈ Friday of August

Isaiah 19:24

Meaning

This talks about the world power at the time and how the first two lost their way and the third Israel will become the inheritance of God for he will use them as a blessing on the earth to reform the others.

4ᵗʰ Friday of August

Isaiah 44:3

Meaning

This refers to the promises God made to Jacob because of the generational covenant God made with Abraham his grandfather.

God Promises To Bring You Blessings

1st Friday of September
Date: _____

2nd Friday of September
Date: _____

Isaiah 55:1 New American
Standard Bible
(NASB)

The Free Offer of Mercy

55 "Ho! Everyone who thirsts,
come to the waters; And you who
have no money come, buy and
eat. Come, buy wine and milk
Without money and without cost.

Joel 2:14 New American
Standard Bible (NASB)

14 Who knows whether He
will not turn and relent
And leave a blessing behind Him,
Even a grain offering
and a drink offering
For the LORD your God?

3rd Friday of September
Date: _____

4th Friday of September
Date: _____

John 1:16 New American
Standard Bible
(NASB)

16 For of His fullness we have all
received, and grace upon grace.

Leviticus 25:21 New
American Standard Bible
(NASB)

21 then I will so order My blessing
for you in the sixth year that it will
bring forth the crop for three years.

Our prayer

When we proclaim the goodness of the Lord, abundant grace will fall upon us.
Yes Lord! You are the King of Kings! You are the Lord of Lords! You are the name
above all names! We claim this promise of blessings today in Jesus name. Amen.

Talk to God:

_____

_____

What do the above verses mean to you?

1st Friday of September

Isaiah 55:1

Meaning

Here they speak of Life in the spiritual aspect, thirsty refers to the Living water to the soul. And it also speak of Life in the physical aspect, and that is what our body needs for sustenance.

2nd Friday of September

Joel 2:14

Meaning

This refers to Gods mercy after you have repented of you sin and God in his kindness might just bless you with provisions for your sustenance.

3rd Friday of September

John 1:16

Meaning

Grace as explained is just enough and imaging receiving double then it becomes abundant. And that's why you should pray for grace upon grace, its shows humility and ambition at the same time.

4th Friday of September

Leviticus 25:21

Meaning

This talks of seasonal blessing which comes like a well-timed investment that yield at the right time.

God Promises To Bring You Blessings

1st Friday of October

Date: _____

Luke 24:51 New American Standard Bible (NASB)

51 While He was blessing them, He parted from them and was carried up into heaven.

2nd Friday of October

Date: _____

Malachi 3:10 New American Standard Bible (NASB)

10 Bring the whole tithe into the storehouse, so that there may be food in My house, and test Me now in this," says the LORD of hosts, "if I will not open for you the windows of heaven and pour out for you a blessing until it overflows.

3rd Friday of October

Date: _____

Nehemiah 9:5 New American Standard Bible (NASB)

5 Then the Levites, Jeshua, Kadmiel, Bani, Hashabneiah, Sherebiah, Hodiah, Shebaniah and Pethahiah, said, "Arise, bless the LORD your God forever and ever! O may Your glorious name be blessed And exalted above all blessing and praise!

4th Friday of October

Date: _____

Proverbs 10:22 New American Standard Bible (NASB)

22 It is the blessing of the LORD that makes rich, And He adds no sorrow to it.

Our prayer

When we proclaim the goodness of the Lord, abundant grace will fall upon us. Yes Lord! You are the King of Kings! You are the Lord of Lords! You are the name above all names! We claim this promise of blessings today in Jesus name. Amen.

Talk to God:

_____

_____

What do the above verses mean to you?

1st Friday of October

Luke 24:51

Meaning

This is a blessing of love. It happens when someone loves you so much that they shower you with love up until the very last moment. They leave you with their blessings.

2nd Friday of October

Malachi 3:10

Meaning

This talks about Giving. Givers never lack, to whom much is given much is expected. When one is given charge of abundance it is not for one's pleasure. Failing to share of the Blessings of God with others is like robbing God.

3rd Friday of October

Nehemiah 9:5

Meaning

This speaks of humility. Even when God has done so much for us that we have abundance and receive accolades we must remain humble and give God all the glory.

4th Friday of October

Proverbs 10:22

Meaning

This talks about our gifts, talents and skills which makes us unique and when our passion drives these gifts/blessings it tends to bring in income and wealth. And for me it never really feels like work because I derive joy from doing this things.

God Promises To Bring You Blessings

1st Friday of November

Date: _____

2nd Friday of November

Date: _____

Proverbs 10:7 New American
Standard Bible
(NASB)

7 The memory of the righteous
is blessed, But the name
of the wicked will rot.

Proverbs 11:11 New
American Standard Bible
(NASB)

11 By the blessing of the upright a
city is exalted, But by the mouth
of the wicked it is torn down.

3rd Friday of November

Date: _____

4th Friday of November

Date: _____

Proverbs 11:26 New
American Standard Bible
(NASB)

26 He who withholds grain, the
people will curse him, But blessing
will be on the head of him
who sells it.

Proverbs 24:25 New
American Standard Bible
(NASB)

25 But to those who rebuke the
wicked will be delight, And a good
blessing will come upon them.

Our prayer

When we proclaim the goodness of the Lord, abundant grace will fall upon us.
Yes Lord! You are the King of Kings! You are the Lord of Lords! You are the name
above all names! We claim this promise of blessings today in Jesus name. Amen.

Talk to God:

_____

_____

What do the above verses mean to you?

1st Friday of November

2nd Friday of November

Proverbs 10:7

Meaning

If you are successful through the blessings of God, people will make you their role model and idolize you, as compared to people with ill-gotten riches.

Proverbs 11:11

Meaning

This talks about location, and how the actions and reputation of people can either glorify or taint the image of a place.

3rd Friday of November

4th Friday of November

Proverbs 11:26

Meaning

This speaks of Greed for financial benefits. Denying people of what they need in order to make more profit is considered good business but it is cruel and wicked, and people who show compassion to others will receive a thank you from the heart and blessings from the Lord.

Proverbs 24:25

Meaning

This talks about Justice, Truth and Honesty. If you have these traits in judgement and do not take side with wickedness, you will receive favor from God.

God Promises To Bring You Blessings

1st Friday of December

Date: _____

2nd Friday of December

Date: _____

Psalm 129:8 New American
Standard Bible
(NASB)

8 Nor do those who pass by
say, "The blessing of the LORD
be upon you; We bless you in
the name of the LORD."

Psalm 133:3 New American
Standard Bible
(NASB)

3 It is like the dew of Hermon
Coming down upon the mountains
of Zion; For there the LORD
commanded the blessing—
life forever.

3rd Friday of December

Date: _____

4th Friday of December

Date: _____

Psalm 24:5 New American
Standard Bible
(NASB)

5 He shall receive a blessing
from the LORD
And righteousness from the
God of his salvation.

Psalm 3:8 New American
Standard Bible
(NASB)

8 Salvation belongs to the LORD;
Your blessing be upon
Your people! Selah.

Our prayer

When we proclaim the goodness of the Lord, abundant grace will fall upon us.
Yes Lord! You are the King of Kings! You are the Lord of Lords! You are the name
above all names! We claim this promise of blessings today in Jesus name. Amen.

Talk to God:

_____

_____

What do the above verses mean to you?

1st Friday of December

Psalm 129:8

Meaning

This talks about people who hate and persecute you, may they not share of the blessing and favor of the lord.

2nd Friday of December

Psalm 133:3

Meaning

This talks about Peace and Unity and how it feels. When there is peace on earth, life will flourish.

3rd Friday of December

Psalm 24:5

Meaning

This speaks of Faith in God. Those who seek Gods face and worship Him and do not worship other gods. They will find favor and protection in the Lord.

4th Friday of December

Psalm 3:8

Meaning

This also talks of the Faith in God. If you keep his words and have complete faith in Him, he will deliver you from every situation and he will provide for you beyond all imagination.

Daily Guide – God Promises To Provide for Your Needs

Our Prayer

Father God, thank you for this promise of
provision. Thank you for the food we eat, the air
we breathe in, the water we drink, the strength
and most of all for Your goodness and mercy.

We pray for provision of the daily needs of our families,
brothers and sisters in Christ, our love ones and friends.
We pray for provision of our Christian missionaries
who are traveling in different parts of world serving
you. We pray for provision of our churches and their
communities. We pray for provision of all your children
in the world lacking in food and daily needs.

We claim these promises of provision
believing you will supply all our needs.

In the name of Jesus we pray. Amen

God Promises To Provide for Your Needs

1st Saturday of January

Date: _____

2nd Saturday of January

Date: _____

1 Corinthians 10:15-17 New American Standard Bible (NASB)

[15] I speak as to wise men; you judge what I say. 16 Is not the cup of blessing which we bless a sharing in the blood of Christ? Is not the bread which we break a sharing in the body of Christ? [17] Since there is one bread, we who are many are one body; for we all partake of the one bread.

Philippians 4:19 New American Standard Bible (NASB)

[19] And my God will supply [a] all your needs according to His riches in glory in Christ Jesus.

3rd Saturday of January

Date: _____

4th Saturday of January

Date: _____

1 Corinthians 10:31 New American Standard Bible (NASB)

[31] Whether, then, you eat or drink or whatever you do, do all to the glory of God.

Exodus 16:12 New American Standard Bible (NASB)

[12] "I have heard the grumblings of the sons of Israel; speak to them, saying, At twilight you shall eat meat, and in the morning you shall be filled with bread; and you shall know that I am the Lord your God.'"

Our prayer

Father God, thank you for this promise of provision. Thank you for the food we eat, the air we breathe in, the water we drink, the strength and most of all for your goodness and mercy. We claim this promise today in Jesus' name. Amen.

Talk to God:

_____

_____

What do the above verses mean to you?

1st Saturday of January

1 Corinthians 10:15-17

Meaning

Jesus explained his actions with the words, 'This is my body.' That is, the bread meant his body. He broke it to show that, soon, he would die on the cross. He told the disciples to eat it because they all needed to benefit from his death. God could save them only because of his death. Paul explained that the single loaf had a special meaning, too. It showed that Christians were not separate people with their own private beliefs. By the death of Jesus, God had joined them together, as if they were one body. We have become a child of God. Then you have nothing to worry about, God is ready to perfect all that concerns you and provide for His children's needs. Amen.

2nd Saturday of January

Philippians 4:19

Meaning

It says that God shall supply all your needs according to his riches in glory by Christ Jesus, this is a divine promise from God to you, why then do you have to worry? God will surely do what He says, so His provision are ready for you. Thank God. Claim this promise.

3rd Saturday of January

1 Corinthians 10:31

Meaning

This verse stimulates the fact that as a Christian in whatsoever you do, must learn to always give thanks and glory to God, by giving God all the glory, He will bless you the more, His promises of provision will be showered on you always. Thank you Lord.

4th Saturday of January

Exodus 16:12

Meaning

Look how good God is. Even the Israelites were grumbling, God provided them food. They do not have to work for it. God gave them meat & bread. Giving thanks to God over everything means referencing him for all that he has done, when you give thanks to God in all things, he is ready to multiply you thereof, no matter the situations that you may be passing through, always give thanks to God, and His promises will never change concerning you. Amen.

God Promises To Provide for Your Needs

Date: _____

Date: _____

Romans 14:23 New American
Standard Bible
(NASB)

23 But he who doubts is condemned
if he eats, because his eating is
not from faith; and whatever
is not from faith is sin.

Romans 14:14 New American
Standard Bible
(NASB)

14 I know and am convinced
in the Lord Jesus that nothing
is unclean in itself; but to him
who thinks anything to be
unclean, to him it is unclean.

3rd Saturday of February

Date: _____

4th Saturday of February

Date: _____

Romans 14:2 New American
Standard Bible
(NASB)

2 One person has faith that he
may eat all things, but he who
is weak eats vegetables only.

---

1 Corinthians 8:8 New
American Standard Bible
(NASB)

8 But food will not commend
us to God; we are neither the
worse if we do not eat, nor
the better if we do eat.

Our prayer

Father God, thank you for this promise of provision. Thank you for the food we
eat, the air we breathe in, the water we drink, the strength and most of all for your
goodness and mercy. We claim this promise today in Jesus' name. Amen.

Talk to God:

_____

_____

What do the above verses mean to you?

1st Saturday of February

Romans 14:23

Meaning

Having faith in God is a key to fulfillment of Gods promises of provisions over your life, do not be doubtful, put your mind at rest and see GOD do wonders for your sake. Amen.

2nd Saturday of February

Romans 14:14

Meaning

Speaking from the very depths of Christian principle as one who knows that he has himself put on the Spirit of Christ. Hence, you must be conscious of yourself about earthly things, whether they are in line with the scriptures or not. By doing this, you become a useful vessel for the Lord. In no time, Gods promises will be fulfilled over your life. Amen.

3rd Saturday of February

Romans 14:2

Meaning

In other, converted Gentile, who rightly understands his Christian liberty, is firmly persuaded that he may eat any kind of food indifferently, though forbidden by the ceremonial law, without sin. Another, who is weak — A believing Jew, not thoroughly informed of his Christian liberty; eat herbs. Ask God for understanding of this principle, He will make you strong, and in Him you will be liberated will all provision that he has in store for you. Amen.

4th Saturday of February

1 Corinthians 8:8

Meaning

The vanities of life. Meat cannot take us closer to God. You only need to do is to enjoy Gods provision is for you to seek his first, and forego worldly things, when you seek Him and subject yourself to Him, He will move closer to you in return and give you all that you need. Thank you Lord.

God Promises To Provide for Your Needs

1st Saturday of March

Date: _____

2nd Saturday of March

Date: _____

---

1 Samuel 17:17 New American Standard Bible (NASB)

¹⁷ Then Jesse said to David his son, "Take now for your brothers an ephah of this roasted grain and these ten loaves and run to the camp to your brothers.

---

1 Timothy 4:4-5 New American Standard Bible (NASB)

⁴ For everything created by God is good, and nothing is to be rejected if it is received with gratitude; 5 for it is sanctified by means of the word of God and prayer.

3rd Saturday of March

Date: _____

4th Saturday of March

Date: _____

Isaiah 1:19 New American Standard Bible (NASB)

¹⁹ "If you consent and obey, You will eat the best of the land;

Acts 27:35 New American Standard Bible (NASB)

³⁵ Having said this, he took bread and gave thanks to God in the presence of all, and he broke it and began to eat.

Our prayer

Father God, thank you for this promise of provision. Thank you for the food we eat, the air we breathe in, the water we drink, the strength and most of all for your goodness and mercy. We claim this promise today in Jesus' name. Amen.

Talk to God:

_____

_____

What do the above verses mean to you?

1st Saturday of March

2nd Saturday of March

1 Samuel 17:17

Meaning

Jesse thought provisions might be scarce with them. But, having other sons at home with him, it was, no doubt, through a divine influence that he sent David from the sheep upon this errand, even than the love of a father to his sons, God do love you, since God is your creator, He knows your needs, and His faithfulness concerning you will never change. Thank you Father God.

1 Timothy 4:4-5

Meaning

Chapter 4 says for every creature of God is good. This particular text shows that God has made you to be in His image, He is pleased with you. Be thankful to God and receive His blessings with gladness. You don't have to worry about anything, as God has given you a divine purpose, and made you good, His provisions for you is forever sure.

3rd Saturday of March

4th Saturday of March

Isaiah 1:19

Meaning

Here, the bible verse says if you are willing and obedient, you will eat the good things of the land. A conditional promise. Bible says obedience is better than sacrifice, heeding to the word of God is the best thing to do, when you walk with God He will walk with you, and once He walks with you, you can never miss it, and of course you will eat the good things of the land and enjoy His blessings.

Acts 27:35

Meaning

Giving thanks to God over everything means referencing Him for all that He has done. When you give thanks to God in all things, He is ready to multiply you thereof, no matter the situations that you may be passing through, always give thanks to God, and His promises will never change concerning you. Amen.

God Promises To Provide for Your Needs

1st Saturday of April

Date: _____

Colossians 2:16 New
American Standard Bible
(NASB)

16 Therefore no one is to act as
your judge in regard to food or
drink or in respect to a festival or
a new moon or a Sabbath day—

2nd Saturday of April

Date: _____

Daniel 1:8 New American
Standard Bible
(NASB)

Daniel's Resolve

8 But Daniel [a]made up his mind
that he would not defile himself
with the king's choice food or
with the wine which he drank;
so he sought permission from
the commander of the officials
that he might not defile himself.

3rd Saturday of April

Date: _____

Ecclesiastes 8:15 New
American Standard Bible
(NASB)

15 So I commended pleasure,
for there is nothing good for
a man under the sun except
to eat and to drink and to be
merry, and this will stand by
him in his toils throughout the
days of his life which God has
given him under the sun.

4th Saturday of April

Date: _____

Psalm 107:9 New American
Standard Bible
(NASB)

9 For He has satisfied
the thirsty soul,
And the hungry soul He has
filled with what is good.

Our prayer

Father God, thank you for this promise of provision. Thank you for the food we
eat, the air we breathe in, the water we drink, the strength and most of all for your
goodness and mercy. We claim this promise today in Jesus' name. Amen.

Talk to God:

_____

_____

What do the above verses mean to you?

1st Saturday of April

Colossians 2:16

Meaning

The real theme of this bible verse started from the 1st verse which was verse 16, it says, let no man therefore judge you, in meat or in drink, or in respect to holidays, or of the new moon, or of the Sabbath. Do not use human as your judge or a controller of your daily needs. Obey GOD as the one who can replenish everything that concerns you. Yes Lord, Amen.

2nd Saturday of April

Daniel 1:8

Meaning

He was cautious from the first. He feared that he might eat something that had been consecrated to idols. When we fear the lord, it is the beginning of wisdom, and of course, fearing God is the most important thing, when you fear Him you are being consecrated, and this makes the blessings of the Lord to be endowed on you, bringing about divine provisions for you.

3rd Saturday of April

Ecclesiastes 8:15

Meaning

It is obvious that you can see God's love over you is paramount. He commended to be joyful, because a man has no better thing under the sun, than to eat, and to drink, and to be merry: God knows your heart, and everything that you desire, it is the truth, and He has created everything just for you, surely this is a strong statement that Gods provision concerning you will surely be effected. Claim this promise.

4th Saturday of April

Psalm 107:9

Meaning

Only God can fill your hungry soul. Come to God for all your needs, He fills the hungry not just physically but spiritually as well. Claim this promise.

God Promises To Provide for Your Needs

1st Saturday of May

Date: _____

2nd Saturday of May

Date: _____

Genesis 1:29 New American
Standard Bible
(NASB)

29 Then God said, "Behold, I have
given you every plant yielding
seed that is on the surface of
all the earth, and every tree
which has fruit yielding seed;
it shall be food for you;

Genesis 1:30 New American
Standard Bible
(NASB)

30 and to every beast of the earth
and to every bird of the sky and to
everything that moves on the earth
which has life, I have given every
green plant for food"; and it was so.

3rd Saturday of May

Date: _____

4th Saturday of May

Date: _____

Genesis 3:19 New American
Standard Bible
(NASB)

19 By the sweat of your face
You will eat bread,
Till you return to the ground,
Because from it you were
taken; For you are dust,
And to dust you shall return."

Genesis 9:3 New American
Standard Bible
(NASB)

3 Every moving thing that is alive
shall be food for you; I give all to
you, as I gave the green plant.

Our prayer

Father God, thank you for this promise of provision. Thank you for the food we
eat, the air we breathe in, the water we drink, the strength and most of all for your
goodness and mercy. We claim this promise today in Jesus' name. Amen.

Talk to God:

_____

_____

What do the above verses mean to you?

1st Saturday of May

Genesis 1:29

Meaning

This bible verse is so direct and full of God's positive declaration over your life, God said, "Behold, I have given you every plant yielding seed that is on the surface of all the earth. He said they shall be food for you, all these are God special plan and purposes for you, and it is a call to remember that you can never lack and Gods provision will continue to abide in you. Thank you Father God.

2nd Saturday of May

Genesis 1:30

Meaning

Herbs and fruits must be man's food, including corn, and all the products of the earth. So cast your care upon him, and not be troubled about what you shall eat, and what you shall drink. He that feeds His birds will not starve you, His provision concerning you will be made manifest. Amen.

3rd Saturday of May

Genesis 3:19

Meaning

Looking at this verse, this is a curse from God to Adam and Eve, they made a mistake and the wrath of God was upon them, Hence our God is a merciful God and full of compassion, it is important for you to know that this curse can be a blessing to you, and Gods provision of His riches will be given to you without having to toil the land and stress yourself, and this can be done, if only you heed to his warnings, hence when you heed to God's warning and you obey His commandments, you should know that you will enjoy all his divine provisions.

4th Saturday of May

Genesis 9:3

Meaning

This is an assurance of God's declaration over your life, and it will be just as He said. You will have plentiful of meat; as well as the green herbs. God have given you all things, His faithfulness is forever sure, and you will receive all these blessings just as He has promised. Thank you God.

God Promises To Provide for Your Needs

1st Saturday of June

Date: _____

Hebrews 13:2 New American
Standard Bible
(NASB)

2 Do not neglect to show
hospitality to strangers, for
by this some have entertained
angels without knowing it.

2nd Saturday of June

Date: _____

Isaiah 55:2 New American
Standard Bible
(NASB)

2 "Why do you spend money
for what is not bread, And
your wages for what does not
satisfy? Listen carefully to Me,
and eat what is good, And
delight yourself in abundance.

3rd Saturday of June

Date: _____

Isaiah 58:10 New American
Standard Bible
(NASB)

10 And if you give yourself to
the hungry And satisfy the
desire of the afflicted, Then your
light will rise in darkness
And your gloom will
become like midday.

4th Saturday of June

Date: _____

Isaiah 7:15 New American
Standard Bible
(NASB)

15 He will eat curds and honey
at the time He knows enough to
refuse evil and choose good.

Our prayer

Father God, thank you for this promise of provision. Thank you for the food we
eat, the air we breathe in, the water we drink, the strength and most of all for your
goodness and mercy. We claim this promise today in Jesus' name. Amen.

Talk to God:

_____

_____

What do the above verses mean to you?

1st Saturday of June

Hebrews 13:2

Meaning

The scripture here urge you to receive the stranger who comes to you who is hungry and lost. You may not know who they are and where they come from but if you feel the need and it is in power to help, do so especially pertaining to food. Consider it an honor and a blessing to give. The influence of such guests in you is worth more than it costs to entertain them. Helping will cause God to promote you, and His provision will manifest over your life.

2nd Saturday of June

Isaiah 55:2

Meaning

Here the key message says "listen diligently to me, and eat you that which is good, and let your soul delight itself in abundance". All you need to do to enjoy Gods promises on provisions. Listen to His promptings in your heart and abide in Him, and all things will be gifted to you, spiritually and physically. Claim this promise

3rd Saturday of June

Isaiah 58:10

Meaning

A conditional promise. Feed the hungry. Can be interpreted as hunger In earthly food and hunger in spirituality. Both will satisfy the one who needs it. When you give up part of yourself for the sake of others, there is a blessing that follows this, there is a promise of Gods provision which awaits you in the end.

4th Saturday of June

Isaiah 7:15

Meaning

This verse is talking about Immanuel, which is our Lord Jesus Christ, The purpose of the verse states that he should be consecrated. He is the Lamb of God. Jesus in his human side will consume food just as we are. As he grows he refuses evil and choose to do good. Follow Jesus, though you hunger for food, hunger also for the word of God. His provision is in your life.

God Promises To Provide for Your Needs

1st Saturday of July

Date: _____

> James 3:17 New American
> Standard Bible
> (NASB)
>
> [17] But the wisdom from above
> is first pure, then peaceable,
> gentle, reasonable, full of mercy
> and good fruits, unwavering,
> without hypocrisy.

2nd Saturday of July

Date: _____

> James 3:18 New American
> Standard Bible
> (NASB)
>
> [18] And the seed whose fruit is
> righteousness is sown in peace
> by those who make peace.

3rd Saturday of July

Date: _____

> Job 10:10 New American
> Standard Bible
> (NASB)
>
> [10] 'Did You not pour
> me out like milk
> And curdle me like cheese;

4th Saturday of July

Date: _____

> John 6:11 New American
> Standard Bible
> (NASB)
>
> [11] Jesus then took the loaves,
> and having given thanks, He
> distributed to those who were
> seated; likewise also of the fish
> as much as they wanted.

Our prayer

Father God, thank you for this promise of provision. Thank you for the food we eat, the air we breathe in, the water we drink, the strength and most of all for your goodness and mercy. We claim this promise today in Jesus' name. Amen.

Talk to God:

_____

_____

What do the above verses mean to you?

1st Saturday of July

James 3:17

Meaning

This verse show the difference between men's pretending to be wise, and their being really so. He who thinks well, or he who talks well, is not wise in the sense of the Scripture, if he does not live and act well. Such wisdom comes not down from above, but springs up from earthly principles, acts on earthly motives, and is intent on serving earthly purposes. So for you to be able to enjoy Gods divine provision, you need to avoid evil, and make yourself upright before the Lord, with this his divine provision will be endowed on you.

2nd Saturday of July

James 3:18

Meaning

This verse talks about making peace and resisting the devil. When you make peace, you tend to follow peace with all men, to be peaceful with everyone is aligned with God's will because it is a key that can be used to propagate the word of God to everyone. By doing this, every point of your needs, God will surely meet you. Thank you Lord.

3rd Saturday of July

Job 10:10

Meaning

Job pleaded with God for mercy. He reminded God that God fed him with milk and cheese. Looking at this meaning, as a Christian and follower of Christ, you should always plead for God's mercy although okay to complain if you are desperate, He knows everything that you desire, and once you subject yourself to Him, He will surely give you that good portion that you deserve.

4th Saturday of July

John 6:11

Meaning

This bible verse is a popular one, and it shows how God is always putting you and I on his mind, he care for us, and know all what our hearts wishes, he surely knows that you need to food to eat among other needs, He will surely give you bread when you need it at the right time. He is faithful and His promises concerning you will be manifested just like when he fed thousands of people. This is a strong confirmation that God is capable of providing you adequate provisions.

God Promises To Provide for Your Needs

1st Saturday of August

Date: _____

John 6:27 New American
Standard Bible
(NASB)

27 Do not work for the food
which perishes, but for the
food which endures to eternal
life, which the Son of Man will
give to you, for on Him the
Father, God, has set His seal."

2nd Saturday of August

Date: _____

John 6:50 New American
Standard Bible (NASB)

50 This is the bread which comes
down out of heaven, so that
one may eat of it and not die.

3rd Saturday of August

Date: _____

John 6:55-56 New American
Standard Bible
(NASB)

55 For My flesh is true food, and
My blood is true drink. 56 He
who eats My flesh and drinks
My blood abides in
Me, and I in him.

4th Saturday of August

Date: _____

Ecclesiastes 9:7 New
American Standard Bible
(NASB)

7 Go then, eat your bread in
happiness and drink your wine
with a cheerful heart; for God has
already approved your works.

Our prayer

Father God, thank you for this promise of provision. Thank you for the food we
eat, the air we breathe in, the water we drink, the strength and most of all for your
goodness and mercy. We claim this promise today in Jesus' name. Amen.

Talk to God:

_____

_____

What do the above verses mean to you?

1st Saturday of August

John 6:27

Meaning

Scripture is consistent in reminding us that we need more than just physical food in order to thrive—we need to be nourished spiritually, as well. This does not mean work has no value or that Jesus is endorsing laziness. Rather, His point is simply that all material things will eventually pass away. Instead of being consumed with things like food and spectacle, you ought to be concerned with eternal rewards. Thank you Lord Jesus.

2nd Saturday of August

John 6:50

Meaning

Jesus offers eternal life. Not just food we eat. if any man eat of this bread he shall live forever; not a natural, but a spiritual life; a life of sanctification, which is begun here, and will be perfected hereafter; and a life of glory, which will never end: hence for you to be able to enjoy Gods provisions you need to go to Jesus he is a living bread, and when you taste from a living bread, you can never go hungry, this is God's plan for you, it has been designed for you, all you need to do is to let Jesus take the lead and you follow.

3rd Saturday of August

John 6:55-56

Meaning

This verse further explains that he who eats the flesh and drinks the blood of Jesus will have eternal life, for he has the true elements of life. Not literally, Jesus symbolizes bread as his body and wine as his blood. This is a communion with our Lord Jesus. Do this as often as you can. Love the Lord Jesus

4th Saturday of August

Ecclesiastes 9:7

Meaning

God is good indeed. He wants you to enjoy your provisions. Of course, giving thanks always to acknowledge God's goodness. Claim this promise. Praise the Lord!

God Promises To Provide for Your Needs

1st Saturday of September

Date: _____

2nd Saturday of September

Date: _____

Leviticus 11:47 New American Standard Bible (NASB)

47 to make a distinction between the unclean and the clean, and between the edible creature and the creature which is not to be eaten.

Luke 12:23 New American Standard Bible (NASB)

23 For life is more than food, and the body more than clothing.

3rd Saturday of September

Date: _____

4th Saturday of September

Date: _____

Mark 14:23 New American Standard Bible (NASB)

23 And when He had taken a cup and given thanks, He gave it to them, and they all drank from it.

Mark 8:6 New American Standard Bible (NASB)

6 And He *directed the people to sit down on the ground; and taking the seven loaves, He gave thanks and broke them, and started giving them to His disciples to serve to them, and they served them to the people.

Our prayer

Father God, thank you for this promise of provision. Thank you for the food we eat, the air we breathe in, the water we drink, the strength and most of all for your goodness and mercy. We claim this promise today in Jesus' name. Amen.

Talk to God:

_____

_____

What do the above verses mean to you?

1st Saturday of September

Leviticus 11:47

Meaning

Before you can be able to please God, you need to differentiate between the unclean from the clean, our God is a clean God, and a holy God, hence for His blessings to be able to manifest in your life, you need to set the difference between the clean and the unclean, by doing this, you follow the true path of righteousness, and at the end Gods promises will be made fulfilled concerning you.

2nd Saturday of September

Luke 12:23

Meaning

Christ largely insisted upon this caution not to give way to disquieting, perplexing cares. The arguments here used are for our encouragement to cast our care upon God, which is the right way to get ease. When you cast your burden upon God, then your life will be changed inside out, you begin to feel the presence of Gods dominion over you, and you will see more to life. Thank you Lord.

3rd Saturday of September

Mark 14:23

Meaning

This is a further explanation that states that in everything give thanks. Thanking God is showing appreciation, even Jesus himself glorifies God always. When you show appreciation, God blesses you more, His provision are been multiplied for your sake. Amen.

4th Saturday of September

Mark 8:6

Meaning

Giving thanks brings about multiplication as stated earlier in the above bible verse, Jesus fed 5,000 (five thousand) with just five loaves of bread and two fishes, for you to be able to enjoy God's promises on provision, you need to give thanks to God for everything He has done for you, doing this, He will bless you continually.

God Promises To Provide for Your Needs

1st Saturday of October

Date: _____

2nd Saturday of October

Date: _____

Matthew 15:11 New American Standard Bible (NASB)

11 It is not what enters into the mouth that defiles the man, but what proceeds out of the mouth, this defiles the man."

Matthew 6:11 New American Standard Bible (NASB)

11 'Give us this day our daily bread.

3rd Saturday of October

Date: _____

4th Saturday of October

Date: _____

Proverbs 15:17 New American Standard Bible (NASB)

17 Better is a dish of vegetables where love is Than a fattened ox served with hatred.

Proverbs 27:27 New American Standard Bible (NASB)

27 And there will be goats' milk enough for your food, For the food of your household, And sustenance for your maidens.

Our prayer

Father God, thank you for this promise of provision. Thank you for the food we eat, the air we breathe in, the water we drink, the strength and most of all for your goodness and mercy. We claim this promise today in Jesus' name. Amen.

Talk to God:

_____

_____

What do the above verses mean to you?

1st Saturday of October

2nd Saturday of October

Matthew 15:11

Meaning

You should know has a Christian that you can be defiled with what comes from your mouth, hence you need to keep your mouth with a bridle, by doing this, you are been consecrated, and once you are been consecrated, you will enjoy Gods promises of provision. Be blessed!

Matthew 6:11

Meaning

Since prayer is the key to all things, then you need to pray and tell God all that you need. Of course He answers prayers, and when He answers your prayer, all His promises concerning you will be influenced in you. Ask God for your daily bread, and you shall receive. Claim this promise.

3rd Saturday of October

4th Saturday of October

Proverbs 15:17

Meaning

Love is something we all should strive for. Jesus is the symbol of that love. Not the monetary value of the food but who you shared the food with and more importantly who provided the food to you. It is God. God's provisions. Thank you Father God.

Proverbs 27:27

Meaning

This is a confirmation of Gods promises over your life on provision, he says that you shall have goats' milk enough for your food, for the food of your household, and for the maintenance for your maidens, and so shall this be for you. Amen.

God Promises To Provide for Your Needs

1st Saturday of November

Date: _____

Proverbs 30:8 New American Standard Bible (NASB) 8 Keep deception and lies far from me, Give me neither poverty nor riches; Feed me with the food that is my portion,

2nd Saturday of November

Date: _____

Proverbs 31:15 New American Standard Bible (NASB) 15 She rises also while it is still night And gives food to her household And portions to her maidens.

3rd Saturday of November

Date: _____

Psalm 104:14 New American Standard Bible (NASB) 14 He causes the grass to grow for the cattle, And vegetation for the labor of man, So that he may bring forth food from the earth,

4th Saturday of November

Date: _____

Psalm 111:5 New American Standard Bible (NASB) 5 He has given food to those who fear Him; He will remember His covenant forever.

Our prayer

Father God, thank you for this promise of provision. Thank you for the food we eat, the air we breathe in, the water we drink, the strength and most of all for your goodness and mercy. We claim this promise today in Jesus' name. Amen.

Talk to God:

_____

_____

What do the above verses mean to you?

1st Saturday of November

Proverbs 30:8

Meaning

This verse is about, Agur who wisely prayed he might be kept at a distance from temptations; he asked daily bread suited to his station, his family, and his real good. There is a remarkable similarity between this prayer and several clauses of the Lord's Prayer. If you are removed from vanity and lies; if you are interested in the pardoning love of Christ, and have him for our portion. When you have contentment with what God has given you, He will continue to elevate you, and always enlarge your coast, His promises will always be made ready for you.

2nd Saturday of November

Proverbs 31:15

Meaning

When you make yourself available to meet the needs of others, you are showing love which is the greatest of all commandment, Jesus is love and he will surely reciprocate your good deeds back to you in multiple folds, he will meet you at the point of your needs just as you have done, and he will make provisions for your desires. Thank you Lord Jesus.

3rd Saturday of November

Psalm 104:14

Meaning

When you reflect upon the provision made for all creatures, you should also notice the natural worship they render to God. Do not forget the spiritual blessings; the fruitfulness of the church through grace, the bread of everlasting life, the cup of salvation, and the oil of gladness. Always remember to be grateful so that the blessing and promises of God will continue to flow in your life.

4th Saturday of November

Psalm 111:5

Meaning

When you fear the lord, you tend to keep all His commandment, and when you keep his commandments there are various blessings that follows with it. He will be mindful of his promises and covenant for you, and you will receive abundant blessings from Him. Claim this promise.

God Promises To Provide for Your Needs

1st Saturday of December

Date: _____

Psalm 145:15 New American
Standard Bible
(NASB)

15 The eyes of all look to You,
And You give them their
food in due time.

2nd Saturday of December

Date: _____

Psalm 23:5 New American
Standard Bible
(NASB)

5 You prepare a table before me
in the presence of my enemies;
You have anointed my
head with oil;
My cup overflows.

3rd Saturday of December

Date: _____

Psalm 34:8 New American
Standard Bible
(NASB)

8 O taste and see that the LORD
is good; How blessed is the man
who takes refuge in Him!

4th Saturday of December

Date: _____

2 Peter 1:3 New American
Standard Bible (NASB)

3 seeing that His divine power
has granted to us everything
pertaining to life and godliness,
through the true knowledge
of Him who called
us [a]by His own glory
and [b]excellence.

Our prayer

Father God, thank you for this promise of provision. Thank you for the food we eat, the air we breathe in, the water we drink, the strength and most of all for your goodness and mercy. We claim this promise today in Jesus' name. Amen.

Talk to God:

_____

_____

What do the above verses mean to you?

1st Saturday of December

2nd Saturday of December

Psalm 145:15

Meaning

Always cast your burden upon the Lord. Fix your eyes on Him, and He will fulfill His promises, and provides for your needs, believe in Him, and you will enjoy His provisions. Claim this promise.

Psalm 23:5

Meaning

The main implication of this verse is that as a believer you need to put your confidence in God's grace and care. When you do so, you are practicing faith, and without faith you cannot please God. Believe in him. Once you put your confidence in God, He is ready to lift you, grant you what your heart desires. And makes core provision all round for your sake. Amen.

3rd Saturday of December

4th Saturday of December

Psalm 34:8

Meaning

This verse says you should put your trust in God. When you put your trust in Him, He will not fail you, you will be blessed. When you are blessed, his provision is been manifested one way or the other in your life. Amen. Claim this promise

2 Peter 1:3

Meaning

God supernaturally have given us everything we need to live a godly life. To be able to understand His commands, a true knowledge. This is so we His children will live in glory and excellence. Claim this promise.

Thank you Father God for everything.

Our Prayer

Father God, thank you for this promise of
peace & joy. We believe that only in trusting
You, we find perfect peace and joy.

We for peace and joy in our own households that parents
and children will understand and accept each other.

We pray for peace in our neighborhoods, in our cities and in
our countries. We pray for peace of those victims of injustices
and fill hearts with forgiveness. We pray to those who are
lonely, feeling abandoned, separated from spouse, broken
relationships, financially down, desperate, lost, and sick or
their love ones come to God and find peace in their hearts.

We claim these promises of peace & joy
believing in Your goodness.

In the name of Jesus we pray. Amen

God Promises to Give You Peace & Joy

1st Sunday of January

Date: _____

> 2 Timothy 1:7 New American
> Standard Bible
> (NASB)
>
> 7 For God has not given us a
> spirit of timidity, but of power
> and love and discipline.

2nd Sunday of January

Date: _____

> Isaiah 26:3 New American
> Standard Bible
> (NASB)
>
> 3 "The steadfast of mind You
> will keep in perfect peace,
> Because he trusts in You.

3rd Sunday of January

Date: _____

> Job 41:22 New American
> Standard Bible
> (NASB)
>
> 22 "In his neck lodges strength,
> And dismay leaps before him.

4th Sunday of January

Date: _____

> Psalm 35:27 New American
> Standard Bible
> (NASB)
>
> 27 Let them shout for joy and
> rejoice, who favor my vindication;
> And let them say continually,
> "The LORD be
> magnified,
> Who delights in the
> prosperity of His servant."

Our prayer

Father God, thank you for this promise of peace & joy. We believe that only in trusting you, we find perfect peace and joy. We claim this promise today in Jesus' name. Amen.

Talk to God:

_____

_____

What do the above verses mean to you?

1st Sunday of January

2 Timothy 1:7

Meaning

A sound mind recognizes that we are special to God, not from our own strength but because of the gift of His Holy Spirit. Even though we may be only one person and insignificant, we must have the kind of mind that takes charge of it and moves forward, not in retreat as many of God's people are doing today. God is a very positive God, who looks forward to the future and the promises of having us as a key part of His creation.

2nd Sunday of January

Isaiah 26:3

Meaning

Understand that your peace is connected to you trusting God. "To have one's mind...stayed "to lean upon," or to be "sustained". This indicates that we as believers must completely and totally trust the Lord. We are to lean entirely on the Lord and be sustained by Him alone. Today, you must make the choice to totally surrender and trust in God. Lean not on your own understanding, but acknowledge Him in all your ways and He will direct your paths.

3rd Sunday of January

Job 41:22

Meaning

The joy of the Lord is both our strength and security. It is a place where you should be, and where God wants you to be. However, there are joy stealers that keep you away from this place of refuge. Two of these joy stealers are grief and depression. There is nothing wrong with grieving over something or feeling sad over a situation. Yet, you should not let this linger longer than it should. The whole of your being craves joy, because to continue living in this negative world you will need strength for each day and the joy of the Lord is your strength.

4th Sunday of January

Psalm 35:27

Meaning

You will notice that joy is right next to love, for without love there is no joy. Without this joy being in your life then there will be no peace in your life. And without this God peace in your life then there will be no long-suffering and patience. Without long-suffering and patience, there will be no gentleness. Without gentleness there will be no goodness exhibited in your life. And without goodness, faithfulness will never be a fruit of your daily life.

God Promises to Give You Peace & Joy

1st Sunday of February

Date: _____

2nd Sunday of February

Date: _____

---

1 Peter 1:8 New American
Standard Bible
(NASB)

8 and though you have not
seen Him, you love Him,
and though you do not see
Him now, but believe in Him,
you greatly rejoice with joy
inexpressible and full of glory,

---

1 Peter 5:7 New American
Standard Bible
(NASB)

7 casting all your anxiety on
Him, because He cares for you.

3rd Sunday of February

Date: _____

4th Sunday of February

Date: _____

---

2 Timothy 1:2 New American
Standard Bible
(NASB)

2 To Timothy, my beloved
son: Grace, mercy and peace
from God the Father and
Christ Jesus our Lord.

Galatians 5:22-23 New
American Standard Bible
(NASB)

22 But the fruit of the Spirit is love,
joy, peace, patience, kindness,
goodness, faithfulness,
23 gentleness, self-control; against
such things there is no law

Our prayer

Father God, thank you for this promise of peace & joy. We believe that only in
trusting you, we find perfect peace and joy. We claim this promise today in Jesus'
name. Amen.

Talk to God:

_____

_____

What do the above verses mean to you?

1st Sunday of February

2nd Sunday of February

1 Peter 1:8

Meaning

We all suffer from seasons of sadness, but that does not mean joy is out of reach. In times of depravity, anxiety, pain and suffering, Jesus Christ awaits us to lay it at his feet so that we may be filled with joy. Claim this promise.

1 Peter 5:7

Meaning

Casting all your care upon Him; for He cares for you, casting the whole of your care--all your anxieties, all your worries, all your concerns, once and for all--on Him; for He cares for you affectionately, and care about you watchfully. As we strive to live the life that God intends we will encounter many obstacles, difficulties and challenges… storms (winds and waves) that we will need to overcome. You need to cast your cares on God.

3rd Sunday of February

4th Sunday of February

2 Timothy 1:2

Meaning

Timothy, my dearly beloved son: Grace, mercy, and peace, from God the Father and Christ Jesus our Lord.
It is only as we recognize our place within the body of Christ and come to the realization that we do each have a specific, important ministry...it is only then that we will find the joy and fulfillment that comes from serving the living Christ. Find courage in others who are great examples of the Christian faith.

Galatians 5:22-23

Meaning

There are things God wants to build in you and to do for you. Many times you tie God's hands because of your ways. Joy and peace is inclusive. The Fruit of the Spirit. Received them all today.

God Promises to Give You Peace & Joy

1st Sunday of March

Date: _____

> Habakkuk 3:18 New American Standard Bible (NASB)
>
> 18 Yet I will exult in the LORD, I will rejoice in the God of my salvation.

2nd Sunday of March

Date: _____

> Isaiah 35:10 New American Standard Bible (NASB)
>
> 10 And the ransomed of the LORD will return And come with joyful shouting to Zion, With everlasting joy upon their heads. They will find gladness and joy, And sorrow and sighing will flee away.

3rd Sunday of March

Date: _____

> Isaiah 51:11 New American Standard Bible (NASB)
>
> 11 So the ransomed of the LORD will return And come with joyful shouting to Zion, And everlasting joy will be on their heads. They will obtain gladness and joy, And sorrow and sighing will flee away.

4th Sunday of March

Date: _____

> Isaiah 55:12 New American Standard Bible (NASB)
>
> 12 "For you will go out with joy And be led forth with peace; The mountains and the hills will break forth into shouts of joy before you, And all the trees of the field will clap their hands.

Our prayer

Father God, thank you for this promise of peace & joy. We believe that only in trusting you, we find perfect peace and joy. We claim this promise today in Jesus' name. Amen.

Talk to God:

_____

_____

What do the above verses mean to you?

1st Sunday of March

Habakkuk 3:18

Meaning

The promise is to supply all your need; in this world where many things you think are sources of joy in your lives, you sometimes mistakenly identify them as the true source of this great emotion. Why not look at God's Word and see what it says about God's Fullness of Joy

2nd Sunday of March

Isaiah 35:10

Meaning

God asks you to keep the long run in view when you consider what is occurring in your life. He works things out in His way on His time schedules. But God will bless His people with peace, productivity, and provision. Joy in Suffering "Only the redeemed will walk there. You are the redeemed of the Lord.

3rd Sunday of March

Isaiah 51:11

Meaning

Security comes to the redeemed from God. Instead of fear, trust in the power that sets free the captives and provides. He is the One who establishes what cannot be broken. Claim this promise.

4th Sunday of March

Isaiah 55:12

Meaning

The enemy of soul oftentimes uses your memories against you. He will use them to distract you from what the Lord is trying to do in your lives. Walking in faith knowing that wither you will feel him near or not. He is at work in your life. God's will for you is to lead you into the Promised Land! And into your inheritance. You will only relax and enjoy the journey if you understand his plan for getting you there. God doesn't think the way you do.

God Promises to Give You Peace & Joy

1st Sunday of April

Date: _____

2nd Sunday of April

Date: _____

Isaiah 61:10 New American Standard Bible (NASB)

[10] I will rejoice greatly in the LORD, My soul will exult in my God; For He has clothed me with garments of salvation, He has wrapped me with a robe of righteousness, As a bridegroom decks himself with a garland, And as a bride adorns herself with her jewels.

Job 22:26 New American Standard Bible (NASB)

[26] "For then you will delight in the Almighty And lift up your face to God.

3rd Sunday of April

Date: _____

4th Sunday of April

Date: _____

Job 33:26 New American Standard Bible (NASB)

[26] Then he will pray to God, and He will accept him, That he may see His face with joy, And He may restore His righteousness to man.

John 15:11 New American Standard Bible (NASB)

[11] These things I have spoken to you so that My joy may be in you, and that your joy may be made full.

Our prayer

Father God, thank you for this promise of peace & joy. We believe that only in trusting you, we find perfect peace and joy. We claim this promise today in Jesus' name. Amen.

Talk to God:

_____

_____

What do the above verses mean to you?

1st Sunday of April

Isaiah 61:10

Meaning

God has a dream for your life!
God has a plan for your life and
all His children. It is a perfect
plan that brings honor and Glory
to Him and blessing to you.
Amen.

2nd Sunday of April

Job 22:26

Meaning

God is telling you to put your
trust in the Lord and all of your
problems would be over. You
need to follow His leading and
allow him to take you through all
you need to be fully furnished,
equip and ready for greater task.

3rd Sunday of April

Job 33:26

Meaning

God is patient toward you and
He has gone to great lengths
to bring you to Himself.
God is warm and
accepting and joyous.
Amen.

4th Sunday of April

John 15:11

Meaning

You are created to be connected
to your God. He demands a
permanent relationship from you.
It is only in Him you can flourish,
be stable and fruitful. There is
not so much out there rather in
Christ. Thank you Lord Jesus.

God Promises to Give You Peace & Joy

1st Sunday of May

Date: _____

> John 16:22 New American Standard Bible (NASB)
>
> 22 Therefore you too have grief now; but I will see you again, and your heart will rejoice, and no one will take your joy away from you.

2nd Sunday of May

Date: _____

> John 16:33 New American Standard Bible (NASB)
>
> 33 These things I have spoken to you, so that in Me you may have peace. In the world you have tribulation, but take courage; I have overcome the world."

3rd Sunday of May

Date: _____

> Leviticus 26:6-7 New American Standard Bible (NASB)
>
> 6 I shall also grant peace in the land, so that you may lie down with no one making you tremble. I shall also eliminate harmful beasts from the land, and no sword will pass through your land. 7 But you will chase your enemies and they will fall before you by the sword;

4th Sunday of May

Date: _____

> Malachi 3:10 New American Standard Bible (NASB)
>
> 10 Bring the whole tithe into the storehouse, so that there may be food in My house, and test Me now in this," says the LORD of hosts, "if I will not open for you the windows of heaven and pour out for you a blessing until it overflows.

Our prayer

Father God, thank you for this promise of peace & joy. We believe that only in trusting you, we find perfect peace and joy. We claim this promise today in Jesus' name. Amen.

Talk to God:

_____

_____

What do the above verses mean to you?

1st Sunday of May

John 16:22

Meaning

Jesus speaks to His disciples about the trials they will face as they fulfill The Great Commission to take the Gospel to the world. But they would not be alone because He would send them another Helper. The Spirit would give them reasons to rejoice and the power to overcome their foes. You will have tribulations but the truth is He has overcome the world for you. trust ih His promises and you will see it manifest in your life.

2nd Sunday of May

John 16:33

Meaning

Sometimes life makes you feel like you are getting punched and we don't have a chance to cover up and defend yourselves. Is this an appropriate analogy of how some of your days go? What can you do when life hurts? There is no peace until you have peace in Jesus. The peace He gives, no one and nothing can give it.

3rd Sunday of May

Leviticus 26:6-7

Meaning

The world is full of troubles and so much turmoil, but there is a place of peace in Christ. Once you've step into this place of peace, nothing else matters again in this World.

4th Sunday of May

Malachi 3:10

Meaning

Understanding the benefits of giving to God and the kingdom is important. Nowhere does it show throughout biblical history that those who willingly and joyously served the Lord with their resources did not receive blessings from God, you will receive harvest to every seed you sow in the kingdom.

God Promises to Give You Peace & Joy

1st Sunday of June

Date: _____

Nehemiah 12:43 New American Standard Bible (NASB)

43 and on that day they offered great sacrifices and rejoiced because God had given them great joy, even the women and children rejoiced, so that the joy of Jerusalem was heard from afar.

2nd Sunday of June

Date: _____

Nehemiah 8:10 New American Standard Bible (NASB)

10 Then he said to them, "Go, eat of the fat, drink of the sweet, and send portions to him who has nothing prepared; for this day is holy to our Lord. Do not be grieved, for the joy of the LORD is your strength."

3rd Sunday of June

Date: _____

Psalm 33:21 New American Standard Bible (NASB)

21 For our heart rejoices in Him, Because we trust in His holy name.

4th Sunday of June

Date: _____

Psalm 105:43 New American Standard Bible (NASB)

43 And He brought forth His people with joy, His chosen ones with a joyful shout.

Our prayer

Father God, thank you for this promise of peace & joy. We believe that only in trusting you, we find perfect peace and joy. We claim this promise today in Jesus' name. Amen.

Talk to God:

_____

_____

What do the above verses mean to you?

1st Sunday of June

Nehemiah 12:43

Meaning

There is no reason in this universe why a Christian should have no joy in life and especially life in Christ. Let the whole world know there is joy in the Lord. If you want to develop joyful generosity, start by giving yourself to the Lord. Then give your songs to the Lord, then your substance to the Lord. When you build with God at the Center, you will overflow with Joy in all Things.

2nd Sunday of June

Nehemiah 8:10

Meaning

Life is filled with challenges. Sometimes along the way, you lose your way and in the process, for one reason or another, you lose your joy or strength, among other things. God promises to restore if you let Him. He is always faithful to restore the lost when you are ready.

3rd Sunday of June

Psalm 33:21

Meaning

The awesomeness of God makes you respect and fear Him, yet His love helps you to hope in Him and no other. Thank you Lord.

4th Sunday of June

Psalm 105:43

Meaning

The Promise of God will lead you to the redemption experience. The Lord who called you out of darkness will lead you to the place of fulfillment if you will allow him to finish what He has started in your life. Just believe him and wait upon his Word and time.

God Promises to Give You Peace & Joy

1st Sunday of July

Date: _____

2nd Sunday of July

Date: _____

---

1 Samuel 25:6 New American
Standard Bible
(NASB)

[6] and thus you shall say, Have a
long life, peace be to you, and
peace be to your house, and
peace be to all that you have.

Psalm 16:11 New American
Standard Bible
(NASB)

[11] You will make known to
me the path of life; In Your
presence is fullness of joy;
In Your right hand there
are pleasures forever.

3rd Sunday of July

Date: _____

4th Sunday of July

Date: _____

Psalm 33:21 New American
Standard Bible
(NASB)

[21] For our heart rejoices in Him,
Because we trust in His holy name.

Psalm 27:6 New American
Standard Bible
(NASB)

[6] And now my head will be lifted
up above my enemies around me,
And I will offer in His tent
sacrifices with shouts of joy;
I will sing, yes, I will sing
praises to the LORD.

Our prayer

Father God, thank you for this promise of peace & joy. We believe that only in trusting you, we find perfect peace and joy. We claim this promise today in Jesus' name. Amen.

Talk to God:

_____

_____

What do the above verses mean to you?

1st Sunday of July

1 Samuel 25:6
Meaning

Do not make yourself enjoy good things of life and gather yourself all riches with the help of devil. He who does these things will not know peace. When you prosper through the power of God you will surely know peace and joy, not only you, your generation will be peaceful as well. Amen.

2nd Sunday of July

Psalm 16:11

Meaning

How content are you with your God-given assignments in life? You have the right to pursue happiness. However, you will soon discover that happiness is fleeting. Joy is better, but how do you find, obtain and keep it? There is not much in the world that you can be assured of anymore. But you can be assured of these things, that Christ in you, is the hope of glory. That is where your joy lies.

3rd Sunday of July

Psalm 33:21

Meaning

Each day you are given a chance to praise Him and honor him. You can reflect back on what He has done and give him honor for it. Trust, and hope in the Lord more. God is worthy to be praised and certainly be trusted.

4th Sunday of July

Psalm 27:6

Meaning

Do you delight in God offers? You should be committed like this as well; do you desire to see Him in every facet of your life? God is your light in darkness, God is your strength when you are weak, and God is your salvation when you need to be delivered.

God Promises to Give You Peace & Joy

1st Sunday of August

Date: _____

Psalm 30:5 New American
Standard Bible
(NASB)

5 For His anger is but for a
moment, His favor is for a lifetime;
Weeping may last for the night,
But a shout of joy comes
in the morning.

2nd Sunday of August

Date: _____

Psalm 32:11 New American
Standard Bible
(NASB)

11 Be glad in the LORD and
rejoice, you righteous ones;
And shout for joy, all you
who are upright in heart.

3rd Sunday of August

Date: _____

Psalm 36:8 New American
Standard Bible
(NASB)

8 They drink their fill of the
abundance of Your house;
And You give them to drink
of the river of Your delights.

4th Sunday of August

Date: _____

Psalm 42:4 New American
Standard Bible
(NASB)

4 These things I remember and
I pour out my soul within me.
For I used to go along with the
throng and lead them in procession
to the house of God, With the
voice of joy and thanksgiving,
a multitude keeping festival.

Our prayer

Father God, thank you for this promise of peace & joy. We believe that only in
trusting you, we find perfect peace and joy. We claim this promise today in Jesus'
name. Amen.

Talk to God:

_____

_____

46-15

What do the above verses mean to you?

1st Sunday of August

Psalm 30:5

Meaning

God will ultimately make you triumphs over death, and sorrow, and wipe all tears away from the face of your lives. You need to trust Him and stay focus in Him. He knows all you are going through and always ready to help you

2nd Sunday of August

Psalm 32:11

Meaning

At one time or another you needed directions to find your way to somewhere. It is no different with God's will for your lives. He has the map you must allow Him to navigate.

3rd Sunday of August

Psalm 36:8

Meaning

When you can start admitting who you are and your focus begins to change from yourselves to God, even in the face of all that you are going through. You still can find refuge in God!

4th Sunday of August

Psalm 42:4

Meaning

The challenges Christian's face is just like that of non-Christians. The difference is that those who put their faith and hope in God have a Savior to lean upon, to guide them and comfort them as they walk through such events. God is present in your joy, your despair, and in your hope.

God Promises to Give You Peace & Joy

1st Sunday of September

Date: _____

Psalm 43:4 New American
Standard Bible
(NASB)

4 Then I will go to the altar of
God, To God my exceeding joy;
And upon the lyre I shall
praise You, O God, my God.

2nd Sunday of September

Date: _____

Psalm 5:11 New American
Standard Bible
(NASB)

11 But let all who take refuge in You
be glad, Let them ever sing for joy;
And may You shelter them,
That those who love Your
name may exult in
You.

3rd Sunday of September

Date: _____

Psalm 51:12 New American
Standard Bible
(NASB)

12 Restore to me the joy
of Your salvation
And sustain me with
a willing spirit.

4th Sunday of September

Date: _____

Psalm 16:8 New American
Standard Bible
(NASB)

8 I have set the LORD continually
before me; Because He is at
my right hand, I will not be
shaken.

Our prayer

Father God, thank you for this promise of peace & joy. We believe that only in trusting you, we find perfect peace and joy. We claim this promise today in Jesus' name. Amen.

Talk to God:

_____

_____

What do the above verses mean to you?

1st Sunday of September

Psalm 43:4

Meaning

God promises you strength. So why do you find yourselves more weak than strong? What can you do to ensure power for every task? Every Christian needs to have a place to meet with the Lord. You will have to learn how to build a life of prayer and dedication to the Lord to generate power.

2nd Sunday of September

Psalm 5:11

Meaning

Joy is the result of faithfully following Jesus Christ. God's gives to His children a word of encouragement especially as they go through difficult circumstances when they learn to love Him and walk in accordance to His purpose.

3rd Sunday of September

Psalm 51:12

Meaning

In order for you to live in the Favor of the Lord, you must position yourselves and align yourselves with Him in all areas of your lives. The Lord wants to bless and favor people who diligently and fervently seek after Him. The Lord envelop the righteous with favor.

4th Sunday of September

Psalm 16:8

Meaning

Regardless of how difficult opposition may rise, remember that Almighty God has a purpose and plan to far exceed anything of the world and its leverages. When you stand firm in the relationship with God, He gives you power to overcome, excel and exceed.

God Promises to Give You Peace & Joy

1st Sunday of October

Date: _____

Psalm 55:22 New American
Standard Bible
(NASB)

22 Cast your burden upon the
LORD and He will sustain you;
He will never allow the
righteous to be shaken.

2nd Sunday of October

Date: _____

Psalm 62:6 New American
Standard Bible
(NASB)

6 He only is my rock and my
salvation, My stronghold;
I shall not be shaken.

3rd Sunday of October

Date: _____

Psalm 118:15 New American
Standard Bible
(NASB)

15 The sound of joyful
shouting and salvation is in
the tents of the righteous;
The right hand of the
LORD does valiantly.

4th Sunday of October

Date: _____

Psalm 126:5-6 New American
Standard Bible
(NASB)

5 Those who sow in tears shall
reap with joyful shouting.
6 He who goes to and fro weeping,
carrying his bag of seed,
Shall indeed come again
with a shout of joy, bringing
his sheaves with him.

Our prayer

Father God, thank you for this promise of peace & joy. We believe that only in trusting you, we find perfect peace and joy. We claim this promise today in Jesus' name. Amen.

Talk to God:

_____

_____

What do the above verses mean to you?

1st Sunday of October

Psalm 55:22

Meaning

God knows this world can be overwhelming and at times it doesn't make much sense at all. To walk in joy you must do four things. Accept where you are in life. Expect a better life ahead. Endure hardships. Embrace your circumstances and fight for what belongs to you in Christ Jesus. He is your peace.

2nd Sunday of October

Psalm 62:6

Meaning

Have you ever had your hope in something crushed – filled with disappointment when you bit into it? Discovered that what you put your faith or trust in was hollow and or empty hope? Jesus proved that He is a Living Hope! So, embrace Him today and find Hope and even joy in the journey! Turn to God for refuge - for healing - for overcoming and for strength.

3rd Sunday of October

Psalm 118:15

Meaning

When times are tough, thank the Lord for His timeless love; trust the Lord for His timely help; and take the Lord in as your triumphant King! Still fear the credit crunch, redundancy, illness, rejection, pain all these things might come, but through the storm through it all remember God is Good, God will not forsake you and leave you and Jesus has paid the price, the Victory is yours. Thank you Lord Jesus.

4th Sunday of October

Psalm 126:5-6

Meaning

Have you ever felt like you lost your joy, do you ever wake up and think... "I used to be happy." Could it be that you joy has been stolen? Don't give up in well doing. You will come back with testimonies; it is just a matter of time.
Amen.

God Promises to Give You Peace & Joy

1st Sunday of November

Date: _____

Psalm 33:21 New American Standard Bible (NASB)

21 For our heart rejoices in Him, Because we trust in His holy name.

2nd Sunday of November

Date: _____

Psalm 4:7 New American Standard Bible (NASB)

7 You have put gladness in my heart, More than when their grain and new wine abound.

3rd Sunday of November

Date: _____

Psalm 63:5 New American Standard Bible (NASB)

5 My soul is satisfied as with marrow and fatness, And my mouth offers praises with joyful lips.

4th Sunday of November

Date: _____

Psalm 64:10 New American Standard Bible (NASB)

10 The righteous man will be glad in the LORD and will take refuge in Him; And all the upright in heart will glory.

Our prayer

Father God, thank you for this promise of peace & joy. We believe that only in trusting you, we find perfect peace and joy. We claim this promise today in Jesus' name. Amen.

Talk to God:

_____

_____

What do the above verses mean to you?

1st Sunday of November

Psalm 33:21

Meaning

The awesomeness of God makes you respect and fear Him, yet His love helps you to hope in Him. Praises to you oh Father God.

2nd Sunday of November

Psalm 4:7

Meaning

Even if terrifying trial would happen to you, as Christians, there are good things that you could expect from your Good God! You are safe because God hears you, you are safe because your trust is in God, and you are safe because God blesses you. His love for you is an everlasting love. Claim this promise.

3rd Sunday of November

Psalm 63:5

Meaning

Even in the midst of trouble, His right hand upholds you. He is the present help in time. God can use the stinky stuff in your lives to help you grow and increase greatly. Even in the midst of trouble, His right hand upholds you.

4th Sunday of November

Psalm 64:10

Meaning

You can come to grips with God's involvement and grace in times of tragedy and suffering. To show that your gladness and glory/victory is in the LORD, you end up giving glory and praise to the LORD.

God Promises to Give You Peace & Joy

1st Sunday of December

Date: _____

2nd Sunday of December

Date: _____

Psalm 68:3 New American
Standard Bible
(NASB)

3 But let the righteous be glad;
let them exult before God;
Yes, let them rejoice with gladness.

Psalm 89:15-16 New
American Standard Bible
(NASB)

15 How blessed are the people
who know the joyful sound!
O LORD, they walk in
the light of Your
countenance.
16 In Your name they rejoice
all the day, And by Your
righteousness they are exalted.

3rd Sunday of December

Date: _____

4th Sunday of December

Date: _____

Psalm 97:11-12 New
American Standard Bible
(NASB)

11 Light is sown like seed
for the righteous
And gladness for the
upright in heart.
12 Be glad in the LORD,
you righteous ones,
And give thanks to His holy name.

Romans 5:1-2 New American
Standard Bible
(NASB)

Results of Justification

5 Therefore, having been justified
by faith, we have peace with God
through our Lord Jesus Christ,
2 through whom also we have
obtained our introduction by
faith into this grace in which
we stand; and we exult in
hope of the glory of God.

Our prayer

Father God, thank you for this promise of peace & joy. We believe that only in trusting you, we find perfect peace and joy. We claim this promise today in Jesus' name. Amen.

Talk to God:

_____

_____

What do the above verses mean to you?

1st Sunday of December

2nd Sunday of December

Psalm 68:3

Meaning

The greatest weapon that you have in the war against the enemy is God himself and when you unite your faith with His Love for you, everything becomes subject to what God wants to do for and in your life. It's not about what you feel; it's never going to be about what you feel, so stop trying once and for all making it about the way you feel. Make it about what you know; what you know God is capable of! And what's God capable of....everything!

Psalm 89:15-16

Meaning

You have got a real reason to praise God; don't ever let anybody tell you otherwise because God is something to get excited about.

3rd Sunday of December

4th Sunday of December

Psalm 97:11-12

Meaning

If you love the Lord as you should what will happen to you? God will not only guard your lives, God will shed light on your path and will bring joy to your heart. You show you love the Lord when you rejoice in awe of his awesome power, when you recognize his righteousness, and when you remember his holiness.

Romans 5:1-2

Meaning

There is no greater love than the love of God that God has for you. There is nothing you can do to make God love you more! There is nothing you can do to make God love you less! His love is Unconditional, Impartial, Everlasting, Infinite, Perfect!

Final Chapter - Claim all the Promises of His Word, and TRUST HIM!

I hope that through reading this book and praying these prayers you have already begun to see God move in your life. I hope that you have seen the value in following God with your whole life, and loving Him with your whole heart. As you wait for God to fulfill His promises, wait with courage, and peace, and patience. Thank Him every day for what He has already given you. Even learn to thank Him for the hard gifts of His loving discipline. Think of a mother or father that says to their child "I don't care what you do. Do whatever you want. It makes no difference to me." The child acts up, and becomes rebellious, getting into trouble, and the parent offers no help, no discipline. This is neglect and abuse. Our kind Father in Heaven takes care to raise us right so that we will be blessed. Trust Him.

Our suffering is momentary, light affliction so look not at the things which are seen, but at the things which are not seen. Trust Him. Trust His Word. Pray fervently, and wait patiently. Care most of all that God produce in you what He has promised to produce, an eternal weight of glory beyond all comparison! Praise the Lord! He is so good, and awesome, and worthy of praise!

My prayer for you is that you get everything God has for you in this life, but especially in the next! Dear reader, surrender your life to Jesus if you have not already. Ask Him to make His home in you and transform you. Have the courage to say "whatever it takes, be glorified in my life." Claim all the promises of His Word, and TRUST HIM!

Let us say a personal prayer of thanks.

> I am thankful Lord for everything that You allow to cross my path. Thankful for the decisions that You allow me to make and the lessons that come from these decisions.
>
> I am thankful, Lord, that I do not have to live under fear anymore, that You have truly set me free, that I am a new creation.
>
> Thankful Lord that You have given me joy unspeakable.
>
> Thankful Lord for the strength and this gift of patience, allowing me to mature in You!
>
> Lord, words do not express my thankfulness.
>
> For Your mighty power is at work in me, transforming me, renewing my mind. To You Lord belongs thanks eternal.
>
> In Jesus' name, amen.

MARIA LOURDES L. FILOTEO, CPA & ASSOCIATES

Accounting Services
Accounts Payables
Payroll Processing
Taxes

1125 West Street
Suite 200
Annapolis, MD 21401

Marilou L. Filoteo, CPA
Phone (410) 575-1118
info@mariafiloteocpa.com
www.mariafiloteocpa.com

MARIA LOURDES L. FILOTEO, CPA
http://mfiloteocpa.com/

Printed in the United States
By Bookmasters